kindle

Welcome...

The ebook is set to revolutionise not only the way we read books and magazines, but the very way they're published. Ten years ago, the idea of a first-time writer having their work read by thousands was a remote possibility. Today, the cost and complexity of publishing have been cut down to size, and literature lovers have a wider choice than ever before.

Amazon has championed digital reading through its keenly-priced Kindles, and an online store through which you can pick up a digital edition of just about any newly-published book at the same time its hardback edition hits the shelves.

In this guide we'll explore this exciting world of digital reading, help you choose the right Kindle for you, and the best case to meet your needs. We'll walk you through downloading books, music and personal documents, answer your Kindle questions and pick out the best sites from which you can download your choice of free content.

Happy e-reading!

Nik Rawlinson

100%

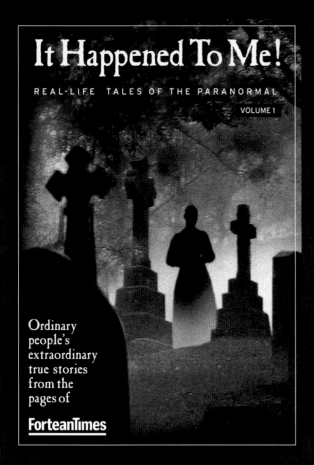
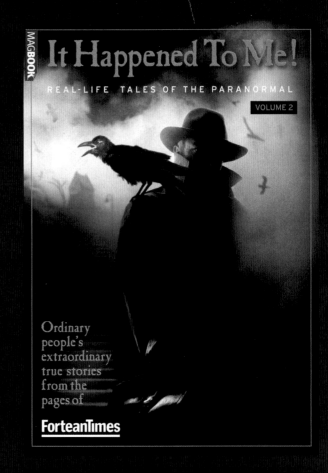
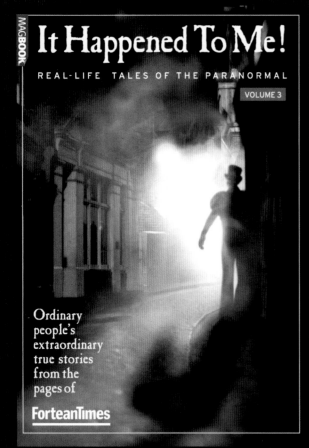
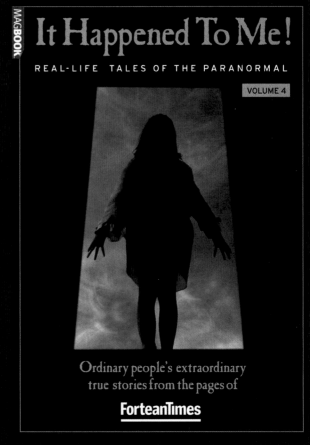

Ultimate Guide to
Amazon Kindle

EDITOR Nik Rawlinson

ADVERTISING
MAGBOOK ACCOUNT MANAGER Katie Wood 020 7907 6689
SENIOR MAGBOOK EXECUTIVE Matt Wakefield 020 7907 6617
DIGITAL PRODUCTION MANAGER Nicky Baker 020 7907 6056

DENNIS PUBLISHING LTD
GROUP MANAGING DIRECTOR Ian Westwood
MANAGING DIRECTOR John Garewal
MD OF ADVERTISING Julian Lloyd-Evans
NEWSTRADE DIRECTOR David Barker
CHIEF OPERATING OFFICER Brett Reynolds
GROUP FINANCE DIRECTOR Ian Leggett
CHIEF EXECUTIVE James Tye
CHAIRMAN Felix Dennis

PUBLISHING AND MARKETING
MAGBOOK PUBLISHER Dharmesh Mistry 020 7907 6100
MARKETING EXECUTIVE Paul Goodhead 020 7907 6012

LICENSING AND REPRINTS

Material in *Ultimate Guide to Amazon Kindle* may not be reproduced in any form without the publisher's written permission. It is available for licensing overseas.

For details about licensing contact Carlotta Serantoni,
+44 (0) 20 7907 6550, *carlotta_serantoni@dennis.co.uk*
To syndicate this content, contact Anj Dosaj-Halai,
+44 (2)20 7907 6132, *anj_dosaj-halai@dennis.co.uk*

Contents

Buying your first Kindle

Reading with your Kindle

10	Complete guide to choosing and buying your first Kindle
12	Kindle
13	Kindle Touch
14	Kindle Keyboard
15	Kindle Fire
16	Kindle competitors
18	The best Kindle cases
22	Setting up and registering your Kindle
23	Security, setting a password and deauthorising a lost or stolen Kindle

26	Buying books directly
28	Sending books to your Kindle from your Mac or PC
29	Adding books by USB
30	Alternative bookstores and downloading free books
34	Playing audio books
36	Highlighting text, making notes and sharing them on social networks
38	How to back up your Kindle purchases
40	Reading your ebooks when you're away from your Kindle
42	Organising book collections
43	Lending and borrowing books

Kindle Fixer

92	Kindle troubleshooter – got a problem with your Kindle you can't solve? Find yourself with a question you can't answer? Here's the first place you should look
96	Kindle glossary. All of the acronyms, jargon and technical terms you need to use – and love – your Kindle. The complete guide to Kindle terminology from 3G to Wireless Access Point

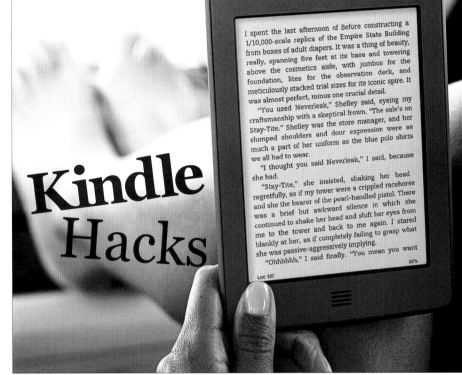

46 How to create and publish your own Kindle books

52 How to sell your digital books through Amazon's online store

56 Hidden Kindle features, including music player, spoken books, a photo gallery application and two games

60 Managing your Kindle remotely

62 Sending documents, including PDFs, to your Kindle

64 Setting up your Kindle to work with Instapaper

Kindle Hacks

Kindle Fire

68 Welcome to Kindle Fire

70 Getting to know, and setting up your Kindle Fire

72 Setting up your Kindle Fire to send and receive email

74 Downloading applications from the Amazon Appstore

76 Downloading, organising and playing music

78 Watching movies

80 Buying and reading books

81 Amazon Newsstand

82 How to work with Amazon Cloud Drive

86 Working on the move with Kindle Fire – using Quickoffice

88 Working on the move with Kindle Fire – synchronising your contacts

Buying your first Kindle

Choosing a Kindle

Buying a Kindle is your first step into an exciting new world of digital reading. You may not believe it right now, but many people who switch from pages to pixels quickly realise that they could never go back, as they're wowed by the convenience of reading on a light, carry-anywhere device.

There's no need to fumble with a bookmark, no chunky volume to weigh down your bag, and a great degree of convenience in being able to both carry a whole library wherever you go and buy new books on the very device through which you'll read them.

Over the years, Amazon has released a whole series of Kindles, with each one smaller, lighter and more powerful than its predecessors. They're keenly priced and offer broadly similar features, and while this may mean whichever you buy will do as good a job as the others of managing and displaying books, it also introduces a degree of confusion because it's not immediately obvious which Kindle might be best for you.

Fortunately we're here to help. On this spread, we'll run through the various features of the four main Kindles to help you get to grips with their differences and identify which one would likely be your perfect reading companion. It's important to get this right, as while you might discard a book when you've finished it, you won't do the same with your Kindle – you'll take it with you as you move on to your next book.

You and your Kindle will spend a lot of time together, so lets take our first look at the family, and start to decide which will suit you best.

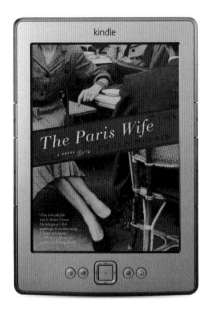

Kindle

Broadly similar to the Kindle touch, but without the touch interface. Navigation is handled by page-turning buttons to the left and right of the casing and a four-way rocker with an action switch in the centre on the face of the device. Further buttons call up the menus, the keyboard and home screen.

To type on the device you must move a cursor around the screen using the four-way controller and press the central button when you get to the character you want. This is very effective, but slower than having a proper keyboard. Some may find it cumbersome.

Sold as a wifi-only reader, there is no wifi/3G version. Available with or without 'offers' in the US, it's available in all of the territories that Amazon sells Kindles. It holds 1400 books, and is the cheapest Kindle on offer – consider it the entry-level device for all Kindle first-timers.

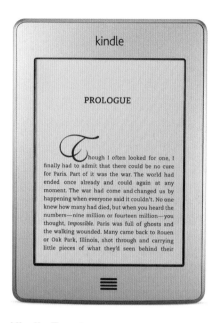

Kindle Touch

Entirely touch-driven Kindle that relies on you pressing relevant parts of the screen to turn pages, purchase books from the online store and navigate its menus.

Uses the same 6in e-ink screen as the regular Kindle and Kindle Keyboard for superiour bright-light performance.

The only possible downside to using this display technology with a touch interface is that using it with grubby fingers could make the display harder to read. Backlit LCDs, on the other hand, help cut through the grime.

Available in wifi-only and wifi/3G versions, the latter of which enables you to buy books when away from your home or office network and works overseas thanks to global roaming agreements. It it, however, unfortunately only available to US-based customers at the time of writing.

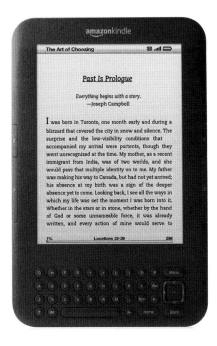

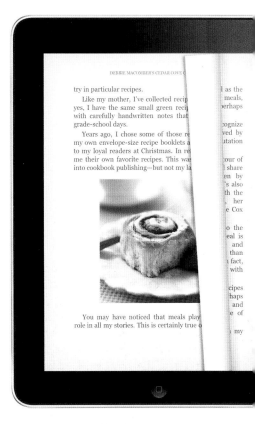

Kindle Keyboard

Previously called the Kindle 3, the Kindle Keyboard is a hang-over from Amazon's last but one line up. It has an important place in the family, though, as it's now the only device on sale to include a hardware keyboard. This will be important for anyone who either doesn't get on with the hunt and peck on-screen keyboard of the Kindle, or doesn't want to physically touch their screen. It greatly eases the process of highlighting, adding notes and searching the store.

Now available only in a wifi/3G version, there is no subsidised edition with 'offers' displayed on screen. Although the body is much larger than the other e-ink devices the screen is still only 6in from corner to corner.

It has a larger memory than the other e-ink editions, too, and is able to store 3500 books at a time for **very** long journeys.

Kindle Fire

Amazon's first proper tablet device is the Kindle Fire. With a touch-sensitive, full-colour 7in display it's the company's challenger to the larger, already market-leading iPad.

Currently only available in the US, it runs an Android-based operating system and Amazon's own Silk browser, which splits the task of downloading web pages between the locally-installed software and Amazon's centralised cloud processing network.

Backed up by a huge library of books, music and movies, and priced very competitively, it looks set to become one of the most important tablet releases to date from anyone other than Apple.

It drops the e-ink display common to the other hardware Kindles in favour of a backlit LCD screen and has sufficient storage for 80 apps, plus 6000 books, 800 songs or 10 movies.

Kindle apps and software

If you already have a PC, Mac, iPad, iPhone, BlackBerry or Android device then you can read Amazon's Kindle books without buying a Kindle device of your own.

Recognising that it can still sell books to non-Kindle owners, it has developed Kindle applications for each of these platforms and made them completely free to download.

Even if you own a Kindle, it's still worth grabbing the apps for any other compatible devices you own, as it means you can carry on reading books where you left off should you leave your Kindle at home.

If you're at work, meanwhile, and want to catch up with your book during your lunch hour, there's also the browser-based Kindle reader, which you can find at *read. amazon.com*. Once you've logged in with your regular Amazon account details, you get access to all your previously purchased material.

Kindle

The entry-level Kindle is the cheapest e-reader Amazon has ever produced.

It's easy to see how the company has managed to make this model of Kindle so affordable: it's seriously stripped down when compared to its siblings, with neither a hardware keyboard nor a touch-sensitive display on offer. There's no 3G option here, so if you don't have a wireless network at home you'll have to either buy your books wirelessly on a public network or at work, or download them to your computer and transfer them using the bundled USB cable. There's also no plug in the box, so if you don't want to buy one as an optional extra you'll have to charge your device by plugging it into a spare USB port on your computer.

American shoppers can cut the cost of buying this most basic of all Kindles still further by opting for the version with what Amazon calls 'special offers'. This translates to adverts, which are displayed on the home screen in place of the standard images that are shown when the Kindle is switched off. The offers don't appear within the pages of your books, so they won't interrupt your reading, and they are genuinely useful in many cases, with past offers including Kindle books for $1 or savings of up to $500 on high definition televisions. These offers are not currently available outside of the US, where shoppers have to pay the full price for their device.

It has a 6in e-ink screen, which is great in bright light but, as is the case with a physical printed book, less effective in dimmer environments. Both Amazon and several third-party manufacturers therefore sell covers with built-in lights that aid reading in the dark. The latest generation of Kindles have a very fast screen refresh rate, which largely overcomes the problem of the flash you see when turning a page.

Although it has the lowest storage capacity of any Kindle in the range, it will nonetheless allow you to carry 1,400 books at any one time, which should be more than enough for even the longest holiday or career break. It also has the lowest-powered battery, yet can keep running for a month on a single charge so long as you read for around half an hour a day and keep the wireless networking features switched off, the only effect of which would be that your current page

	with offers	without
UK	-	£89
US	$79	$109
Screen	6in, 16-level greyscale e-ink display	
Capacity	2GB internal storage, capable of holding 1,400 books	
Comms	Built-in wifi networking plus bundled USB lead	
Formats	Supports Kindle AZW, text, PDF, Mobipocket and PRC formats	
Battery	1 month reading time	
Size	166 x 114 x 8.7mm	
Weight	170g	

position and bookmarks won't be constantly updated online.

As with the other Kindles, it can download books in less than 60 seconds and they'll be backed up in Amazon's cloud system so you can download your purchases again in the future whenever you choose. It has adjustable text sizes and three fonts to choose from and can share highlights and notes online, so long as you're prepared to use the four-way controller to hunt about the on-screen keyboard when tapping out your jottings.

Kindle Touch

One step up from the basic Kindle is the Kindle Touch. It looks very similar to the entry-level device, but look more closely and you'll see that the control buttons at the bottom of its front surface have been dropped, as have the forwards and backwards page turning buttons that sit one above the other on either side of the body. To use it, you instead interact directly with the screen, as you would with a regular tablet device.

This will appeal to many users, as it's a method of control that we are all becoming inherently used to thanks to the proliferation of the touchscreen smartphones flooding the market. However, if you're going to be touching your Kindle's screen on a regular basis it's important to make sure that you're using it with clean fingers. Why? Because the e-ink based Kindles, of which this is one, rely on using reflected light to make their pages legible, and so if you have a lot of dirty fingerprints over the surface of the display you'll reduce the amount of light that can be reflected. The LCD-based Kindle Fire, which is the only other Kindle to rely on having your fingers interacting directly with the on-screen interface, is back-lit, so reflected light isn't so important.

The Touch has sufficient internal capacity to hold around 3000 books, as 3GB of the installed 4GB remains free for use after the operating system has been accounted for. It's a greyscale device, capable of differentiating between 16 different levels of grey. This doesn't sound like much, but when you take into account the fact that it dithers each of these tones in a pattern to imitate a far broader spectrum it's actually very effective.

The battery is more powerful than the one found in the plain Kindle, and in regular use, which Amazon counts as being around half an hour of reading a day with the wireless networking features turned off, you can expect to get around two months' use out of a single charge. Again, this Kindle isn't shipped with a power adaptor so you'll have to either charge it by plugging it into an available USB port on your computer or buy an optional adaptor add-on. Charging through a USB port takes around four hours to complete.

This is the lowest-priced Kindle to include the option of 3G connectivity in addition to the standard wifi feature that appears on all other Kindles. There are no

	with offers	without
UK	-	-
US	$99 (wifi) $149 (3G)	$139 (wifi) $189 (3G)
Screen	6in, 16-level greyscale e-ink display	
Capacity	4GB internal storage, capable of holding 3000 books	
Comms	Built-in wifi networking plus bundled USB lead. Optional 3G.	
Formats	Supports Kindle AZW, text, PDF, Mobipocket and PRC formats	
Battery	2 months reading time	
Size	172 x 119 x 11mm	
Weight	213g	221g

ongoing fees associated with this service, even when you're roaming, allowing you to download a new book wherever you happen to be, even if you don't have access to a local wireless network.

Unfortunately at the time of writing the Kindle Touch is only available to US customers. It's not uncommon for Amazon to ship products only to the US following their initial introduction, so it may yet be rolled out worldwide.

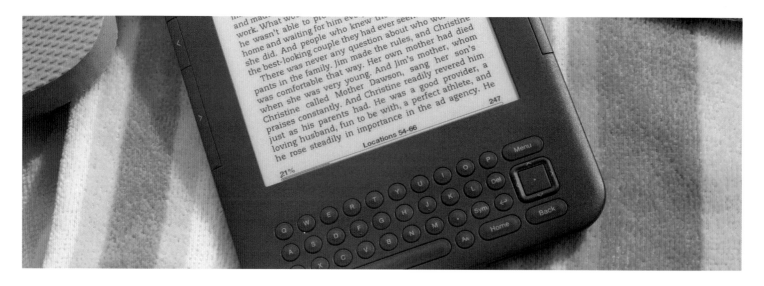

Kindle Keyboard

The headline product from the previous Kindle line-up lives on as part of the ever growing family, albeit with a slightly different name. The Kindle Keyboard was previously known as the plain old Kindle 3, first appearing in 2010 and marking a significant shrinking down in physical size of Amazon's hardware e-reading devices.

Along with the plain Kindle, it's one of only two products that Amazon currently sells outside of the US, and it's by far the more versatile of the two. Despite shipping in a larger case it has the same 6in e-ink screen, but extends the Kindle feature set to offer 3G networking in addition to regular wireless Ethernet, and doubles the storage capacity from 2GB to 4GB. Because the operating system that keeps it running isn't much larger in this device, it has more than twice the amount of free space left over, allowing you to increase the number of books you can carry at any one time from 1,400 to a massive 3,500, which should be enough for even the most vociferous reader on the longest sabbatical.

The biggest and most noticeable difference, though, is the fact that this is the only Kindle with a physical keyboard. Its keys may be fairly small, but it makes a significant difference to the useability of the device, particularly when searching the online store and tapping out short notes relating to the content of your current book.

Look closely and you'll also notice that the page turning buttons, which sit on either side of the casing, are also larger on the Kindle Keyboard than they are on the regular, plain Kindle. This makes them easier to press, and some users will find this a physically more comfortable and convenient Kindle to hold for extended periods.

The Kindle Keyboard ships in a larger box to make room for a bundled power adaptor. This is a significant boon for anyone who doesn't want to have to resort to charging their device by plugging it into a free USB port on their computer, and anyone who thinks they might need to charge it while they're away from home, as it means you won't have to splash out extra on the optional charger that Amazon sells as an add-on for the Kindle and Kindle Touch.

A single charge should see you through two months of reading if you keep the networking features

	wifi + 3G
UK	£149
US	$139
Screen	6in, 16-level greyscale e-ink display
Capacity	4GB internal storage, capable of holding 3,500 books
Comms	Built-in wifi networking plus bundled USB lead. 3G.
Formats	Supports Kindle AZW, text, PDF, Mobipocket and PRC formats
Battery	2 months reading time
Size	190 x 123 x 8.5mm
Weight	247g

turned off and read for an average of two hours a day. The 3G connection has no ongoing fees.

It may not be the latest, greatest addition to the Kindle family, but for our money the Kindle Keyboard remains perhaps the best, most versatile Kindle, and we're very happy to see it live on in this latest iteration. We would, however, have liked to see Amazon keep the wifi-only version around for those readers who don't envisage needing to buy books while away from home.

Kindle Fire

The Fire is the odd one out in the Kindle family, as it's actually a full-blown tablet rather than a simple e-reading device.

It jettisons the other Kindles' 6in greyscale e-ink screens in favour of a 7in, 1024 x 600 resolution, full colour display which, like the Kindle Touch, is fully touch-sensitive, allowing for far greater control.

It also does away with the simplistic operating system that underpins the rest of the Kindle family, swapping it out for a more capable Amazon-tuned variant of Android, the Google-originated OS that runs many smartphones and tablet computers. This means it can access a whole world of third-party applications, which you can download direct from the Amazon Appstore. In this way you can augment the applications that are already installed upon arrival.

Under the hood there's a powerful dual-core processor and 8GB of internal memory. Using Amazon's own calculations, that's enough to store 80 applications alongside 800 songs, 10 full-length feature films or 8,000 books.

Content is downloaded wirelessly using the built-in wifi networking features, but it lacks Bluetooth support, which would allow you to add an external keyboard or wireless headset, and the 3G connectivity option featured on the Kindle Touch and Kindle Keyboard, so when you're away from your home or office network – or a public network – you won't be able to browse the web or send emails.

As with the Kindle Keyboard, Amazon includes a power adaptor in the box. However, because of the screen technology and underlying hardware a single charge will last you a lot less time on the Fire than on any other Kindle device – specifically around eight hours if you're reading and seven and a half if you're playing back video.

This second metric is an important consideration as the Fire looks set to be the biggest challenger yet to Apple's market-leading iPad 2, thanks to the extensive range of content available for the device direct from Amazon, the only company that can realistically compete with the iTunes Store and Apple App Store.

To this end, Kindle Fire owners have access to 10,000 movies and TV shows, an unrivalled online book store, including 5,000 free books, and 17 million songs. It also gives access to the Amazon Cloud service, which is an online home for all of your content, allowing you to store documents and files, and re-download any of the content you have bought in the past without paying for it a second time.

The Fire is really a Kindle in name only. If all you want to do is read books, turn back a page or two.

	wifi-only
UK	-
US	$199
Screen	7in, colour LCD display
Capacity	8GB internal storage, capable of holding 80 apps plus 10 films, 800 songs or 6,000 books
Comms	Built-in wifi networking plus bundled USB lead. No optional 3G.
Formats	Supports Kindle AZW, text, PDF, Mobipocket, PRC, Audible, DOC, DOCX, AAC, MP3, Midi, OFF, Wav, MP4, VP8 and others
Battery	8 hours reading or 7.5 hours video playback
Size	190.5 x 119.5 x 11.5mm
Weight	414g

Kindle competitors

Amazon's Kindle range may well be the best-known line-up of e-reading devices available, but they're far from the only ones. Neither was the first Kindle the earliest e-reader on sale: Apple's readers have simply carved themselves a niche as some of the best supported and widest used readers worldwide.

Choosing an e-reader is about far more than just picking the best hardware for your needs. As each one is usually tied into a dedicated online store you should also consider the price of the books on sale and the size of the range on offer. There's no point buying into a poorly-supported platform, after all.

Each of the e-readers in the line-up here is well supported by an extensive online library, and they also use the widely adopted ePub format for their books, which means it's possible to buy books from rival stores and load them onto each one. That's less often the case with the Kindle, which uses a variation on Mobipocket as its native format and, to date, isn't compatible with ePub.

There is an added advantage to using ePub, which is that more libraries support the format. At the time of writing, library lending is only compatible with the Kindle in the United States, meaning that UK readers who want to borrow books to reduce the cost will have to opt for one of these alternatives.

Each of these devices is available in regular retail stores, with the Sony Reader making it easy to buy books from traditional high street retailers' online shops, giving them a library to rival that offered by Amazon.

Apple iPad 2

The Kindle Fire's strongest competitor is also the world's best-selling tablet computer. The iPad 2 is significantly slimmer than its predecessor and does more than just render books: it's a fully-fledged mobile computer with a backlit 1024 x 768 resolution display, on-screen keyboard, capacities of 16GB to 64GB and both wifi and 3G options. A full charge of the battery lasts around 10 hours.

eBook reading is handled by the free iBooks application, which is tied in to Apple's dedicated iBookstore. This has a narrower selection of books than Amazon, with Apple putting the number of titles on sale at 'over 200,000 and counting', but you can still be pretty sure that any new release you can buy on the Kindle is also available in iBooks.

Amazon had produced a software version of the Kindle for use on the iPad, iPhone and iPod touch, allowing you to read your existing Kindle books on the iPad, arguably giving you the widest possible choice of reading matter.

Price £399 to £659 / $499 to $829
Link www.apple.com/ipad

Sony Reader

The Sony Reader Wi-Fi uses the same e-ink technology as the Kindle, Kindle Touch and Kindle Keyboard. It can store up to 1,200 books or documents in its internal memory and has a MicroSD card slot for expanding its capacity, allowing you to travel with an unlimited number of books at your disposal.

The screen is 6in diagonally from corner to corner and the device itself is 8.8mm thick and weighs a mere 168g. It comes in three colours – black, red and silver – with a 1 month battery life, which matches the entry-level Kindle.

The screen is touch-sensitive; you swipe to turn from one page to the next, and pinch or unpinch, as you would on the iPad, to zoom out and in. As well as the regular British and American English dictionaries it has five built-in translation dictionaries.

You can buy books directly from high street retailers' online stores and, thanks to its ePub compatibility, borrow books from your local library.

Price From £129 / $129
Link www.sony.com/reader

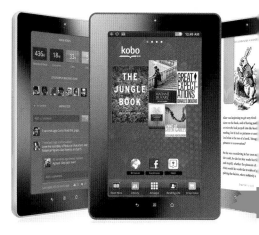

Kobo eReader Touch

Don't let the Kobo eReader Touch's conventional looks fool you; flip it over and you'll find a quilted back for a highly comfotable reading experience (available in blue, silver and black).

Like the Sony Reader, the eReader Touch has a 6in e-ink screen, and wifi connectivity, letting you download books wirelessly. There's one button on the front, which takes you to the home screen, and a SD card slot on the side to expand its capacity. The screen is touch-sensitive, allowing you to turn pages by swiping or tapping.

The Kobo Store has over 2.4 million books in its catalogue, and with ePub support you can also borrow books from your local library.

An interesting Life Stats feature lets you track your reading time, how far you have got through your library and what your reading habits are. You'll also win awards for reading; the more you read, the further you'll progress, with a link to Facebook for bragging rights.

Price From £100 / $99
Link www.kobobooks.com/touch

Kobo Wireless eReader

The Kobo Wireless eReader has a 1,000 book capacity plus an SD card slot for expanding this to 11,000 titles, courtesy of a 32GB memory card – enough for a lifetime of reading.

By Kobo's own measurements, its battery life is 10 days, which is significantly lower than the one-month battery life offered by an entry level Kindle. There's USB and wifi, with the associated bookstore providing access to over two million books (it comes pre-loaded with 100 free classics).

It can read only ePub and PDF documents, so a narrower selection than its competitors, but this does mean it's compatible with local lending libraries. When you consider the low cost of buying the device in the first place and the cost of digital books, this means you can quickly offset the purchase price by borrowing books online rather than buying them.

Altogether, this represents a great value introduction to digital reading.

Price From £69 / $79
Link www.kobobooks.com/wifi

Kobo Vox

The Vox is Kobo's answer to Amazon's Kindle Fire. With a 7in colour screen optimised for reading in bright light and, thanks to its wide viewing angle, shared reading between two people. It has built-in wifi for buying and downloading books, and 8GB of internal storage. There's also an SD card slot for increasing memory capacity. Built on the Android platform, it's extensible with a choice of over 15,000 free applications on offer.

Its associated book store gives you access to over 2.2 million titles, including more than 1 million free books, each of which can be rendered in colour.

As you'd expect of a device that swaps the e-ink screen for a colour display, the battery life is only seven hours when used with the wifi module switched off.

The Vox itself comes in a choice of four colours – hot pink, lime green, ice blue and jet black – and has the same quilted back as other Kobo readers, meaning it's incredibly comfortable to hold.

Price From £169 / $199
Link www.kobobooks.com/kobovox

Perfect protection: Kindle cases

Remember when you used to cover your books in sticky backing plastic? With ebooks, that fiddly habit is a thing of the past. Instead, revel in dressing up your literary friend in one of these smart cases, providing both great protection and a stylish new look.

Here we've picked out what we consider to be the best Kindle cases on offer, with a choice of leather, immitation leather, fabric and natural finishes.

Your Kindle is an important investment, and more than simply a gadget you'll dispose of a few years down the line. Treat it well and it'll reward you with years of faithful service.

A case not only provides that vital protection; it also lets you personalise your device, giving it a feeling of quality and uniqueness we might otherwise risk losing in our haste to swap print for pixels.

Sleek Jacket case and stand for Amazon Kindle 4
£18 / tuff-luv.com
This neat, lightweight case is bundled with a screen protector, allowing you to do away with the cover. Around the back you'll find a neat stand to prop up your Kindle so you can read hands-free if you're busy with other jobs. Available in a range of colours, including the eye-catching 'Lavender' purple seen here.

**Natural Hemp case for
Amazon Kindle Touch**
£25 / tuff-luv.com
Tuff Luv calls this colour Desert Sand,
and it's easy to see why. The thick
fabric is finished with detailed stitching
in the corners and along the spine,
and there's a document holder inside.

**Natural Hemp Brown case
for Amazon Kindle Keyboard**
£20 / tuff-luv.com
This case makes great use of available space,
with room not only for the larger Kindle Keyboard
but also paper and business cards courtesy of the
integrated pouch. There's also pen holder, so even if
you never tap out reading notes on the Kindle itself,
you can write them longhand.

Van Gogh Sky Kindle Cover
$64 / oberondesign.com
Pair your Kindle with one of Oberon
Design's many beautiful leather
cases. Each is handmade and
finished with a pewter buckle. Your
Kindle is secured using marine-
grade bungee straps, and the
screen protected by 100% wool felt.

Manor Bindery KleverCase
£24.99 / klevercase.co.uk

These beautiful reproduction book covers (*left*) are crafted from wibalin card and genuine bookbinding paper, making a lightweight, yet secure case. Your Kindle is held very firmly in place by a moulded surround through which you can still press the page turn buttons. Available for all Kindle models they come in a choice of classic titles to suit any taste and do a great job of disguising your expensive reader on public transport, too.

Maroo Paraoa and Koto
Leather Folio Kindle cases
£29.99 / accessoryvillage.co.uk

We love the tartan and leather finish on these cases (*below*). They're hinged at the top to flip back on themselves so you can use the integrated hand strap to carry them securely, or prop them up for hands-free reading courtesy of the slot on the back cover.

iGadgitz Neoprene Case
£9.99 / igadgitz.com

This simple zip around case (*left*) comes in a choice of colours, and is padded to keep your e-reader secure. It's not moulded to fit the Kindle like a glove, as many others are, so if you choose to switch to a rival reader, you can take it with you. At this price it's also a fair old bargain.

How to register your new Kindle

If you buy your Kindle directly from Amazon it will already be set up, registered to your account and ready for use.

If you bought it from a supermarket, electrical store or other high street shop, however, it won't have any of your details to hand and you'll have to add them yourself by stepping through the easy registration process.

Registering your Kindle isn't simply a means of giving your data to Amazon so that it can send you offers and emails, as you may consider to be the case when you register other software or electrical appliances. Instead, registration is an essential part of setting up your device and preparing it for use. It ties it to your Amazon account so that all of your payment details and gift vouchers will be available to use when you purchase books directly through the device.

The Kindle uses Amazon's one-click purchase system, whereby clicking the Buy Now button on a

Skill level	Beginner – a simple task that everyone can complete
Time required	Around five minutes
Equipment required	Kindle, Kindle Touch, Kindle Keyboard or Kindle Fire, plus Mac or PC with an active network connection and Internet browser

book's listing page immediately buys and downloads the title (although if you bought it by accident, so long as you haven't started reading it you can easily cancel the download, remove the book from your device and receive a refund).

To facilitate registration, every Kindle is assigned a unique serial number. Press the menu button and select Settings and you'll find yours at the bottom of the screen (press *Settings | More | Device* to find it on Kindle Fire). If you have a Kindle Keyboard you can find it by holding shift and alt and pressing full stop.

This pulls up a blank screen with two barcodes and your unique serial number (grab 1, below). Keep this secret and don't share it with friends, but make a note of it for use in the next step.

Now log in to your Amazon account using a regular browser and click *Kindle | Manage Your Kindle | Register a Kindle* (you'll find the last link in the left-hand menu box) to start the process of tying your new Kindle to your existing Amazon account.

Type the serial number you noted from your Kindle menus into the Serial Number box and click *Register*. This ties your Kindle to your account and authorises it to make purchases using your debit or credit card.

Registering in this way not only lets you buy books, but also send documents to your Kindle over email (see p60), and send books from Amazon's site using a regular browser rather than the Kindle (see p28).

Security

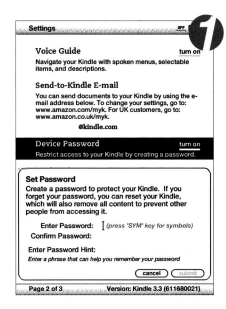

Nobody wants to lose their Kindle; worse still to have it stolen, but it's a sad truth of life that no matter how careful you are with your posessions there's always a chance they will go astray. Fortunately Amazon makes it relatively easy to protect your Kindle and its contents so that even if you don't manage to recover it you can keep prying eyes from any private and personal documents you may have synced to it.

Setting a password

1. Click the menu button and select Settings. Press the page forward button to advance to the next screen. Move down to Device Password and click the centre button.

2. Enter a password that you'll find easy to remember but anyone else would be hard pushed to guess. You should try to use a mixture of letters and symbols or numbers here. On the Kindle Keyboard, use the Sym button to switch to these; on the Kindle and Kindle Touch use the tabbed keyboard to switch to other letter sets. When you have entered a password, add a hint that will help you recall what it is if you later forget it.

3. The next time you switch on your Kindle – and every time thereafter until you deactivate the password – you'll be asked to enter your code before you can do anything. If you have forgotten what your password is, press the down button on the four-way controller. This will reveal your hint, as well as the contact numbers you'll need to get Amazon to reset the device should you have forgotten the password.

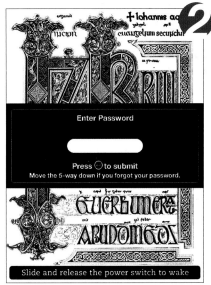

Removing a Kindle from your Amazon account

Should you sell or lose a Kindle, you should deregister it quickly, as this removes it from your account and stops the person you sold it to – or whoever stole it – from buying books using your payment details.

To do this, use a regular browser to log in to Amazon as usual and then click the *Your Account* link above the search bar. Scroll down to the Settings panel and click *Manage Your Kindle*. You'll probably need to enter your password again.

Click *Manage Your Devices* to open a list of all the Kindle hardware devices that you own and have registered to your account, along with any Kindle reader applications installed on smartphones, tablets, Macs or PCs.

Click the *Deregister* link beside each of the devices you want to remove from your account.

Amazon will warn you that you should only deregister a device or application if you are passing it on and that if you do this it will no longer be able to purchase new books on your account. Click *Deregister* to confirm the action.

Reading with your Kindle

Buying books directly

One of the best things about the Kindle platform is its simplicity. No Kindle device needs to be attached to your PC or Mac before it's put to use, and you don't need either of the above to download books, either. You simply unbox the product, charge it up, switch it on and go. The Amazon Kindle Store is built right in to each Kindle device, with an option on the main menu taking you to the store to search for books. Although you can't buy Kindle versions of every book published, the catalogue of available titles is extensive and impressive, and there are several hundred volumes that are available *only* on the Kindle and not in print.

In recognition of the fact that when you're buying a digital book you aren't costing the publisher anything in terms of printing and shipping costs, many Kindle books are cheaper than their regular paper-based editions, allowing you to make significant savings. However, shop carefully, as this isn't always the case and, particularly if you're happy to buy second hand, you can sometimes find physical formats of the same titles for less money.

Here we'll walk you through the process of buying a book directly from your Kindle without the use of a computer as an interim platform. Over the pages that follow we'll show you how to do the same without a wireless connection, and how to send books directly from the Amazon store through a regular web browser. Whichever method you use, you really can be reading books in 60 seconds, just as Amazon promises.

Skill level	Beginner – a simple task that everyone can complete
Time required	Around five minutes
Equipment required	Kindle, Kindle Touch or Kindle Keyboard, including previous generation devices

STEP BY STEP

1. Make sure your Kindle is connected to your network by switching on wifi or using 3G. Return to the menu and select *Shop in Kindle Store* to visit Amazon's optimised shop, containing only Kindle books, through the built-in browser. Use the search box at the bottom of the page to enter the title of your book, the name of a chosen author or keywords relating to the subject you want to read about. Press the centre button to perform the search.

2. When you've found the book you were looking for you can either buy it directly or download the first few pages for free. Do the latter by moving the selector to the *Try a Sample* line and pressing the centre button. The sample will download automatically.

3. You'll be able to read around 5% of the book in this free sample. When you get to the end of the excerpt you can either keep it and take no action or, if you enjoyed it, download the rest of the book. Do this by moving the pointer to the *Buy Now* link and clicking the centre button. So long as your Kindle still has a connection the book will start to download.

4. When the download completes your book will be added to the top of your home screen.

QUICK TIP

Don't forget to check out Amazon's constantly updated lists of most popular books. There are two of these: both paid-for titles and free volumes, each of which can be accessed from the homepage of the Store.

If you're feeling guilty about not being better read in the classics, head for the freebies first as many of the best-loved literary masterpieces are now out of copyright and free to download. It makes a lot more sense to catch up on what you're missing this way, than to head to a regular shop and pay for a physical copy.

Screen 1

Nik's Kindle

amazon.co

Browse:

Books   Blogs

Newspapers

Magazines

Kindle Bestsellers - *The Hanging Shed*

New & Noteworthy Books - *The Payback*

Kindle Post Mon, March 14, 2011 9:36 AM GMT

The Independent
Katy Guest on *A Widow's Story* by Joyce Carol Oates: "This is the first memoir that Oates/Smith has written, and it is...

Recommended for You

See All

| my word is my bond | 🔍 search store |

Screen 2

Nik's Kindle

My Word is My Bond: The Autobiography
by *Sir Roger Moore*

The quintessential suave hero, Roger Moore has enjoyed a successful career that has spanned seven decades, from early television through the golden age of...   *More*

Digital List Price: £6.59
Print List Price: £8.99
Kindle Price: £4.61 (includes VAT)
You Save: £4.38 (49%)
Delivery via *Amazon Whispernet*
Unlike print books, digital books are subject to VAT.

Buy

Try a Sample

Add to Wish List

51 Customer Reviews :   ★★★★☆

Sales Rank: #2,650 in Kindle Store
Text-to-Speech: Enabled
Print Length: 432 pages
Published: Oct 26, 2009
Publisher: Michael O' Mara Books

Customers who bought this book also bought:

★★★★☆ Nerd Do Well , by *Simon Pegg*   See more

| *Begin typing to search* | 🔍 search store |

Screen 3

Annotating is disabled for sample content
buy v. (buys, buying; past and past participle bought) [with obj.] **1** obtain in exchange for payment: *m*

him.

He must have thought I was a real twit!

Once I had recovered, my friends at the lido in Brockwell Park who, in the main, were all older than me, took me across the road from the park to a pub. Underage and never having had anything stronger than one glass of cider, I opted for a glass of mild and bitter. I drank it quickly, before the landlord had a chance to spot this rebel teenage drinker. Before I knew it, I had another pint bought for me and maybe another one after that – things were getting a little hazy and I lost count.

End of this sample Kindle book.
Enjoyed the sample?

Buy Now or

See details for this book in the Kindle Store

100%

Screen 4

Nik's Kindle Keyboard

Showing All 50 Items   By Most Recent

My Word is My Bond: The Autobiography

sample Just As I Am: The Autobiogr...   Billy Graham

sample The Science of Getting ...   Wallace D. Watt...

War and Peace   graf Leo Tolstoy

sample Gravity   Tess Gerritsen

audible Rapid Spanish: Volume 1   Earworms Learning

Kindle intro   nik@nikrawlinson.com

Uncle Tom's Cabin   Harriet Beecher Stowe

World War Z   Max Brooks

The Sketchbook of John, C...   Nik Rawlinson

Page 1 of 6

How to buy books through your desktop's browser

Good though the Kindle's built-in Store is, it's not always the most convenient route through which to buy digital books. If you'd prefer a more leisurely shopping experience, and you have access to a regular computer with an active internet connection, you might instead want to do your shopping through a full browser, and then send your books to your Kindle over the air. Here we'll show you how to do just that in four simple steps.

Skill level	Beginner – a simple task that everyone can complete
Time required	Around five minutes
Equipment required	Any Kindle, including previous versions, and a PC or Mac with an internet connection

STEP BY STEP

1. Open your browser and visit your country's Amazon store. Use the links on the left of the homepage to visit the Kindle Store, selecting *Kindle eBooks* from the fly-out menu. Click in the search box at the top of the page and enter the title of the book you want to read, the name of a favourite author or keywords that describe the subject you're looking for.

2. Select the book you want from the list of results to call up a full description of the publication, an image of the cover and any reviews left written by previous readers.

3. Use the drop-down menu on the right of the screen to select the device to which you want to send the book. This list includes not only regular Kindle hardware devices but also Kindle applications that you've installed on mobile devices such

as the iPhone or iPad, and the reader applications for use on PCs and Macs.

4. Press the menu button on your Kindle and select *Sync & Check for Items* to download the book sent from your browser. You can also send samples by using the *Try it free* drop-down.

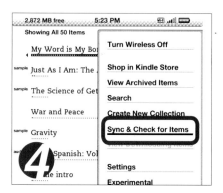

How to transfer books to your Kindle using USB

Over the next few pages we'll be exploring alternatives to the regular Kindle Store. Not only does expanding the number of shops from which you buy content increase your choice of books, but it means you can often find books for free that aren't stocked in the Kindle Store. If you have downloaded books through your browser rather than through Amazon's own store you'll need to transfer them to your Kindle manually by connecting it to your PC or Mac and dragging them over.

Skill level	Beginner – a simple task that everyone can complete
Time required	Around five minutes
Equipment required	Any Kindle, including previous versions, and a PC or Mac with an vacant USB port, Kindle USB cable

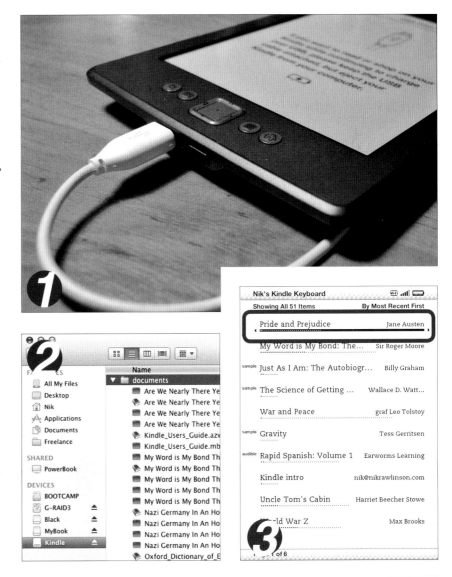

STEP BY STEP

1. Start by connecting your Kindle to your PC or Mac. Ideally you should connect it to a powered port physically attached to your computer, unless any additional external hub connected to your computer has its own power supply. If you've lost the cable that came with your Kindle and need to buy a new one, search Amazon using the term '*usb cable for kindle*' to view authorised replacements.

2. Your Kindle will appear on either your PC or Mac as though it was an external hard drive, with the name Kindle. Here we are using a Mac. Open a Finder or Windows Explorer window and click the Kindle and open the '*documents*' folder.

3. Drag your downloaded Kindle or Mobipocket format book into the folder to send it to your device. It will now appear at the top of your home screen.

QUICK TIP

Always make sure you safely eject your Kindle from your PC or Mac before disconnecting the cable.

Alternative bookstores

Although Amazon's own store is certainly the most convenient place to shop, on account of being intimately tied to the Kindle itself, there are plenty of alternative sources well worth checking out.

By shopping around you can often make savings by downloading cheaper versions of the same books, and in some cases enjoy wider choice, as Amazon's extensive catalogue certainly doesn't include every book ever written converted for Kindle reading.

Here we'll profile the best places to buy books outside of Amazon's walled garden. If you want to go hunting for further options then make sure the books you download are either dedicated .AZW Kindle files, or Mobipocket-formatted books. Amazon's own format is a variation on Mobipocket.

Sadly the widely-used ePub format, which was adopted by Apple as the basis of its own iBook Store, isn't compatible with the Kindle, despite hints that the latest raft of hardware devices would indeed read and render the format.

Don't be tempted to copy paid-for books from friends and family. Not only is this unfair on the authors who in many cases have spent years working on their tomes, but there's a good chance you'll find that the books won't work on your device anyhow. It's also illegal.

Most books downloaded from Amazon and other online bookstores include a digital rights management (DRM) code that ties them to the account of the person who bought them. If that isn't you, they won't work on your Kindle, wasting you both time and digital space.

Project Gutenberg
www.gutenberg.org

Gutenberg is the king of all alternative online book sources. At the time of writing it contains over 36,000 books in a wide range of formats in languages as diverse as Esperanto, Breton and Occitan. All of them have one thing in common: they are out of copyright in the US, and so as long as you're not infringing any copyright regulations in your own country you're free to download them and read them at your leisure.

Project Gutenberg was established by Michael S Hart on 4th July 1971. Appropriately enough, considering the date, the first work he entered into the project's now vast collection, was the Declaration of Independence. At the time he wanted the complete catalogue to eventually hold at least 10,000 of the most commonly consulted books so that they could be accessed and used by anyone for free (although donations remain welcome).

It was a noble cause that over the years has received significant donations and now far exceeds its original stated aims, with an average of 50 new books being added to the database every week.

The most commonly-published language on the site is English, followed in turn by French, German, Finnish, Dutch, Portuguese and Chinese.

Project Gutenberg has a comprenensive search tool allowing you to search the catalogue in a similar manner to Amazon itself, and it maintains a list of newly-

Below: Project Gutenberg is one of the biggest catalogues of free books available on the web, with many in Kindle format.

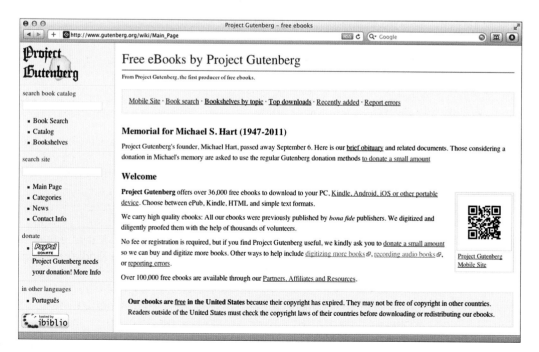

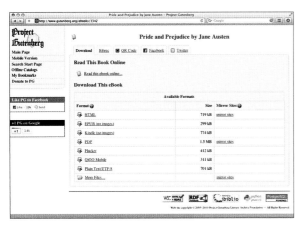

Above: Open a book's dedicated page from the results list and you'll be offered a choice of formats. Choose Kindle if available, and plain text or Mobipocket if not.

added content and most popular downloads if you need a quick fix. This is the best place to look if you're after literary classics, as titles like *Ulysses*, *Jane Eyre* and *Pride and Prejudice* are habitual inhabitants on the list.

To download a book, click its title to open its dedicated record and then choose the format you're after. The simplest of all formats is Plain Text, which is fully compatible with the Kindle, but for the best experience you should choose the Kindle (no images) format if it's offered. Avoid choosing ePub as this won't work on the Kindle – it's intended for alternative hardware readers, and many e-reader apps installed on tablets and smartphones.

Click the appropriate format and if it's one that your browser can't render within its own window it will be downloaded to your computer (you can't send them direct to your Kindle). Follow our instructions on

Chapter 1

It is a truth universally acknowledged, that a single man in possession of a good fortune, must be in want of a wife.

However little known the feelings or views of such a man may be on his first entering a neighbourhood, this truth is so well fixed in the minds of the surrounding families, that he is considered the rightful property of some one or other of their daughters.

"My dear Mr. Bennet," said his lady to him one day, "have you heard that Netherfield Park is let at last?"

Mr. Bennet replied that he had not.

1%

Above: All books are added to the Project Gutenberg catalogue by volunteers and although quality is generally very good stylistic points will vary between the different titles on offer.

page 29 for transferring the file to your Kindle.

You'll find that the quality of the books varies, although in general they're all very well produced and, due to the large number of proofreaders helping out around the world, are generally accurate copies of the original work. They are fully compatible with the Kindle's various options for changing font faces and text size, although obviously you can't remove elements like double spaces (*see grab, above*) that shouldn't be there.

Johannes Gutenberg

Gutenberg, after whom the project is named, is famous for having invented the modern printing press. Living in Mainz in the early 15th century, his innovation was so-called movable type, which allowed the various parts of a page – the letters, numbers and so on – to be moved around and re-used between jobs. The biggest and most famous book printed this way was the Gutenberg Bible, of which 21 copies survive.

Open Library

www.openlibrary.org

The goal of Open Library is to produce a single web page for every book ever published. By its own admission this adds up to 'hundreds of millions of book records'.

Each book's record includes a short review, a picture of the cover and details of each edition published – both digital and physical. These are linked directly to the shops through which you can buy them including Alibris, Amazon, AbeBooks and Book Depository. For our needs, the one that's obviously of greatest interest is Amazon.

So why would you choose to find books this way rather than buy them directly through Amazon? Because it's the easiest way to find out more about your book before you set out to read it. On Amazon you can read the publisher's blurb and, often, reader reviews. Through Open Library, on the other hand, you'll also find excerpts from Wikipedia, information about the different imprints and reprints and comment from such notable experts as Margaret Atwood, and an extensive system of tags and links that put each book in context.

All of the content on the Open Library is open source, from the written words to the underlying code. Like Wikipedia it relies to a great degree on input from a community of volunteers who write and edit each entry. If you find it of use, do your bit by adding some details on and about the last book you enjoyed.

ManyBooks

www.manybooks.net

ManyBooks claims to offer 'the best ebooks at the best price: free'. Its library currently comprises 29,000 titles.

Almost more impressive than the list of books on offer is the range of formats in which they can be downloaded. As well as Kindle AZW and the compatible Mobipocket (.mobi and .prc) formats it has dedicated editions in PDF and plain text (both of which work on the Kindle) and ePub, HTML, RTF, Sony Reader and more.

More than half a million people visit ManyBooks every month, so it's also a great outlet for would-be authors to promote their work through, as ManyBooks also publishes original digital fiction. If you know anything about writing or publishing then you can earn some money – the site is looking for contributors to write on this subject, and is paying a modest fee to those who help out and go on to have their contribution published on the site.

DOWNLOADING FROM MANYBOOKS

Turn on your Kindle's wifi and click Menu > Experimental > Web browser. Visit *mnybks.net* and use the search box to find the author or book you want to download. Click on the *Kindle / Mobipocket* option and confirm that you want to download the file (see grab, below). Once downloaded it will be added to your Home screen. Finish by closing the browser and switching off wireless.

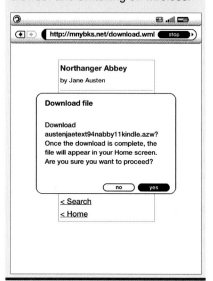

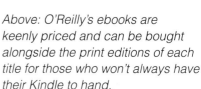

Above: O'Reilly's ebooks are keenly priced and can be bought alongside the print editions of each title for those who won't always have their Kindle to hand.

O'Reilly Media

shop.oreilly.com/category/ebooks.do

O'Reilly is one of the leading publishers of technical non-fiction. Its titles have long been trusted by those who work with computers and web technology as some of the most reliable texts on a wide variety of subjects. Its policy where ebooks are concerned is very liberal and forward-thinking. For starters, it doesn't apply digital rights management measures to its work, meaning there's nothing to stop you from installing them on several of your devices.

It publishes in a wide variety of formats optimised for different platforms (it publishes in Mobipocket format for Kindle-using customers), and it also provides free updates for life, so you know that even if you buy a book today and it receives an update tomorrow you'll be able to download the amendments, too, so that your book stays relevant.

It's worth checking in at the site frequently as it runs deals of the day, so even if the book you're after isn't on offer right now there's a chance it'll appear be before too long.

Feedbooks

www.feedbooks.com

Although Feedbooks' commercial titles aren't compatible with Kindle readers, or their equivalent apps and software installations, its public domain books will work on them. Many of these titles are the same as the books you can find on Project Gutenberg, but the process of searching and downloading through Feedbooks is much more pleasant thanks to a well thought-out interface. It may well be the most successful store you've never heard of, distributing 3,000,000 books a month.

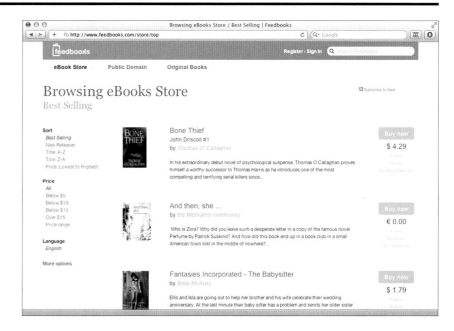

Listening to audiobooks

As we'll show you later (*pp56 - 58*), sound-enabled Kindles can read books aloud, using the text of the book itself, and its integrated speech synthesiser to translate the content into spoken word.

If you have a Kindle Keyboard, Kindle 1, 2 or 3, or Kindle DX you can go one stage further and also play back original spoken word books for which you don't own the text edition, courtesy of downloads from Audible.

Audible books use a specific format that makes them far more flexible and versatile than regular MP3 files. Your Kindle will be able to remember where you left off when you were last listening to one, and you can skip backwards and forwards to specific points. With MP3s, all you can do is play them in the background while you're reading your book (again, *see pp56 - 58*).

Audible sells audiobooks in a number of audio formats, with formats 2 and 3, which are compatible with the first generation Kindle, equivalent to AM and FM radio respectively. Format 4, which is compatible with the first, second and third generation Kindles, plus Kindle DX, is roughly equivalent to an average MP3. Finally, Audible Enhanced Audio has sound quality equivalent to a CD, and is

compatible only with the Kindle DX and second and third-generation devices, including Kindle Keyboard.

Transferring content

Compatible Kindles have an '*audible*' folder ready for you to drop in your content (if yours doesn't and it's listed above, you can create it).

You can only play back Audible files with the .aa or .aac extension. Dropping in any others will have no effect as they won't show up on your Home screen.

Playing audio files

Having successfully transferred your content, eject your Kindle and disconnect it from your computer. You'll see the new file on the Home screen, with 'audible' in the margin to show that it is an audio file. Open it and use the four-way controller's centre button to click the Play button on the transport bar at the bottom of the screen.

If this is the first time you have played an Audible file on your Kindle it will ask you to authorise your device by entering your Audible username and password. If you can't remember what these are, visit *audible.com* or *audible.co.uk*, click Sign in and use the *Forgotten your*

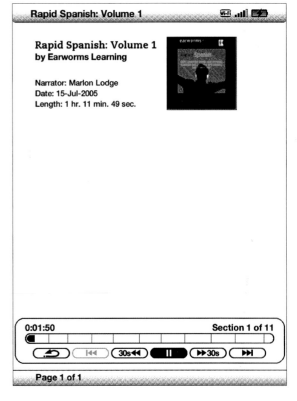

Above: Audible files are encoded in a way that makes them more flexible than MP3s. Many Kindles can make use of this encoding to offer a full set of playback controls.

username or password? link to retrieve them.

You will only need to authorise your device once and it will then play all of your compatible previous purchases on your Kindle.

Left: Kindle Keyboard users, and anyone with an older Kindle device, can buy audiobooks from Audible and play them back using their device's integrated player. Audible is an Amazon company, so it's not surprising that you can link your Amazon and Audible accounts.

QUICK TIP

Not all Audible files are shipped in format 4, so shop carefully. In particular pay attention when buying Audible files through third-party retailers, which may not specify the format on offer.

Highlighting text and posting to social networks

You can't scribble in the margins of a digital book, so Amazon has implemented a clever system of notes and highlights, which allow you to perform a similar task using your Kindle's keyboard controls, and then share them with friends and followers.

Highlighting text

A true bookworm enjoys not just the story, but also the style of the writing contained within its pages. Few who fall into this category can resist the urge to make a note of their favourite passages, but without easily accessible page numbers or the option of turning down a corner you might think that's easier said than done where Kindle books are concerned.

Fortunately not. Every time you come across a notable passage, use the four-way controller on the Kindle and Kindle Keyboard, or touch the screen on the Kindle Touch, and press the centre button. Now move the cursor through the text until you get to the end of the passage. Press the centre button again to save the highlight.

Retrieving your jottings

Your highlights and notes are stored alongside your book and automatically backed up on Amazon's servers (you can turn this off through *Settings | Annotations Backup | turn off*). You can retrieve them by pressing Menu while reading any page of the book and selecting *View Notes & Marks*, where they'll be organised into a table in page order.

she had collected in a small plain trunk, and locking it, desired her husband to see it in the carriage, and then proceeded to call the woman. Soon, arrayed in a cloak, bonnet, and shawl, that had belonged to her benefactress, she appeared at the door with her child in her arms. Mr. Bird hurried her into the carriage, and Mrs. Bird pressed on after her to the carriage steps. Eliza leaned out of the carriage, and put out her hand,--a hand as soft and beautiful as was given in return. She fixed her large, dark eyes, full of earnest meaning, on Mrs. Bird's face, and seemed going to speak. Her lips moved,--she tried once or twice, but there was no sound,--and pointing upward, with a look never to be forgotten, she fell back in the seat, and covered her face. The door was shut, and the carriage drove on.

What a situation, now, for a patriotic senator, that had been all the week before spurring up the legislature of his native state to pass more stringent resolutions against escaping fugitives, their harborers and abettors!

Our good senator in his native state had not

Click to end highlight, ⊕+⊙ to tweet/share, or Back to cancel

Above: To highlight favourite passages from a well-loved book, position the cursor at the start of the passage, press the centre button and then move to the furthest end of the passage before pressing the button again to save it in your stored highlights.

Below: To hide popular highlights, press return while viewing the page on which they appear. Turn them off permanently through Settings.

Popular highlights

If you have chosen to share your highlights with other readers, Amazon will amalgamate them anonymously, along with everyone else's, and sync them along with every copy of the book to which they relate on every device to which it has been downloaded.

These highlights have a feint dotted underline below them in the flow of the book, at the start of which is a note of how many people have chosen to mark it out (*below*). If you find this annoying, turn off the popular highlights feature by opening *Settings*, turning to the second (Kindle Keyboard) or third page (Kindle / Kindle Touch) and clicking the *turn off* link beside Popular Highlights. Just below this you'll also find the link to turn off Public Notes, which are those notes written by people whom you follow at *kindle.amazon.com*. These differ from highlights in that highlights are merely marked out passages of the original text, which are displayed on your device whether you follow the people who marked them out or not.

There are in this world blessed souls, whose sorrows all spring up into joys for others; whose earthly hopes, laid in the grave with many tears, are the seed from which spring healing flowers and balm for the desolate and the distressed. Among such was the delicate woman who sits there by the lamp, dropping slow tears, while she prepares the memorials of her own lost one for the outcast wanderer.

630 highlighters

Set up Kindle to post to Twitter

1. Open *Settings | Social Networks | Manage.* Kindle opens its integrated browser. Select Twitter as the service you want to authorise (*below left*).
2. Enter your Twitter username and password and then click *Sign in* to authorise the application to post to your account (*below right*).
3. You'll be logged in to Twitter and then directed back to the set-up screen which will confirm that the process has completed by displaying your Twitter username within the Twitter section.

If you don't want to turn off the number of popular highlights permanently, pressing return hides them on the current page.

Posting your highlights to Twitter

Whether you want to prove how well read you are, or you just want to inspire your friends to pick up a book you've enjoyed, Kindle also lets you share your favourite passages with your Twitter and Facebook followers using its built-in tools.

To do this it obviously needs to know your login details for each service, so with wifi or 3G active on your device, open Settings and follow the instructions on the panel to the right.

You can now share content from your book using either social media network, remembering at all times to respect any copyright regulations that may be applicable, such as sharing only a small part for the purpose of evaluation or review.

To do this, repeat the process of highlighting your chosen passage by clicking at the start and end of the selected text, and then press alt and return to share it to either network. Kindle will ask you to add a short note to be added to your highlight. When you've done this, click the on-screen '*share*' button. If wifi or 3G are turned on (it'll warn you if they aren't) it will post your covering note to either or both of your social networking accounts, depending on which you have set up, along with a link to the highlighted text, as stored on *kindle.amazon.com*. Linking in this way rather than including it directly allows you to highlight more than Twitter's 140 character limit.

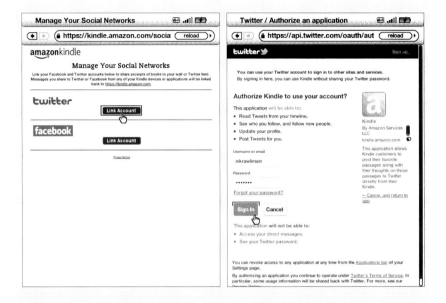

Set up Kindle to post to Facebook

1. Repeat step 1, above, this time choosing to authorise Facebook.
2. Use your email address or phone number to log in to Facebook, remembering that the @ symbol is found behind the SYM button on the Kindle Keyboard, and on the secondary on-screen keyboards on Kindle and Kindle Touch.
3. In an effort to improve security, Facebook likes to register each device you use to access its services. Choose a logical name for your Kindle (we've chosen 'kindle keyboard', *below*) and then confirm that you want it to access your basic information and data and post to Facebook as though it was you by clicking *Allow* on the following screen.

How to back up your Kindle purchases

Keeping a local backup of your Kindle purchases will let you re-install them on your device without downloading them again from Amazon's servers, in the event of a catastrophic crash. Here's how to do it.

Skill level	Intermediate – within the abilities of most users
Time required	Around 20 minutes
Equipment required	Kindle, Kindle Touch or Kindle Keyboard, including previous generation devices, plus PC or Mac

Step by step

1. Use the USB cable that came in your Kindle box to connect the device to your computer. What happens next depends on whether you're using a Mac or PC. On a Mac, the device will appear in the Finder sidebar, and be called Kindle; on a Windows PC it'll be assigned a drive letter. If your PC asks you what you'd like to do with the Kindle, simply choose to open it and it will be treated as though it was a connected external drive.

2. You'll see three default folders on your Kindle: *documents*, *audible* and *music*. The second and third of these contain audio books and MP3s. The first of them – *documents* – is where the Kindle saves your downloaded books. Double-click it to open up its contents. The files inside this folder aren't particularly well organised as your books, their metadata and any text files, PDFs and screen grabs are all bundled together. We only want to back up our books, so use the Mac's toolbar search box to filter it down to just .azw files, or click the drop-down menu on the right hand side of the Type column header in Windows 7 and select AZW as the displayed file types.

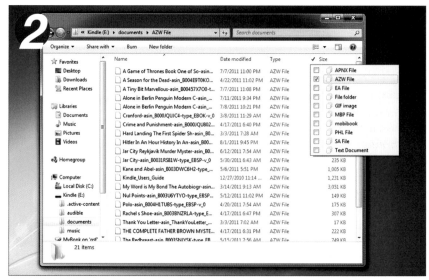

You can now drag these files to another location on your computer to back them up. This will save only the books themselves. If you want to also save your bookmarks then you should also make a copy of any files bearing the same name with a .mbp extension. Store them on a hard drive or flash drive, but don't be tempted to share them with friends.

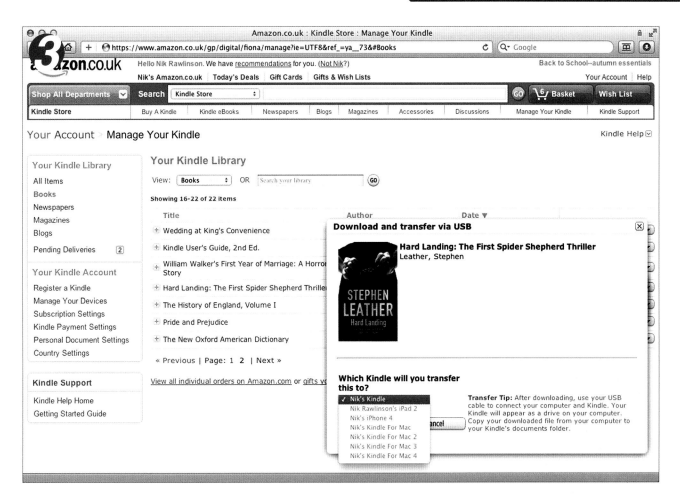

3. Should you have a problem with your Kindle that causes it to lose your books, you can copy them back over USB. However, to read them on an alternative device or an app you'll have to send copies to each one. Do this either by browing through archived items on your Kindle or by logging in to Amazon and selecting *Your Account | Manage your Kindle*. This will call up a list of your past purchases with action buttons beside each one, allowing you to send a previously purchased book to an alternative device.

4. You can also transfer books by USB, which allows you to save money by buying a wifi Kindle even if you don't have a wireless network. To do this, select Transfer by Computer when buying a book and again select the destination device.

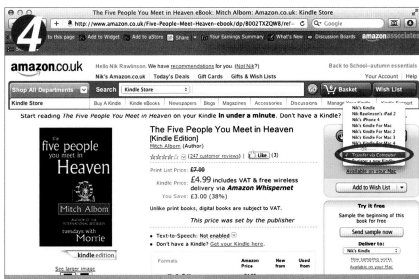

Right: Although you can copy books from your Kindle to local backups for repopulating your device without redownloading all of your books, the digital rights management built in to each one means you can't share them with others.

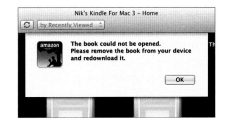

Reading Kindle books ... without using your Kindle

Amazon no doubt turns a tidy profit from the Kindle, but the real money is in books. For every Kindle the company sells, it'll have to remove the cost of research, design, production and shipping before it makes any money. So, too, with paper-based books, which cost money to send through the post.

With a digital book, though, its takings are almost all profit, which is why Amazon can afford to pay its publishers such a generous share of the royalties. All it needs to do is host the book file on its cloud servers and deliver it to the reader whenever they request a copy. The first time they do, the cost of delivery is deducted from the publisher's share of the takings.

It's no wonder, then, that Amazon has sought to push its Kindle technology onto as many platforms as possible, with native applications for the iPad and iPhone, Android phones and Macs and PCs.

Unfortunately for Amazon, Apple changed the rules on in-app purchases for all applications hosted on the iPhone or iPad, dictating that all such purchases should be handled by its own payment processing mechanism, with cards linked to its own online store used as the payment mechanism. Apple would then take 30% of the purchase price to handle processing.

Clearly this was unacceptable to Amazon for two reasons. First, it meant that it lost its direct relationship with its customers, so would find it more difficult to make recommendations to each of us about which books we might enjoy in the future on the basis of what we've bought in the past. Second, the 30% that Apple was demanding in exhchange for processing the purchase was exactly the same as the amount that Amazon took from the sale of each book from its publisher. In one fell swoop it would have wiped out all of the profit that Amazon could have expected to make on each book sale through the iPhone, iPad and iPod touch.

Apple gave its app developers a fair amount of notice that it intended to implement this process, and that applications which didn't comply could no longer be sold through its online App Store. Amazon duly developed new apps for Apple's mobile devices and

Below: Native apps let you read Kindle purchases on a Mac or PC

Where to download a Kindle app for your device

Android phone
https://market.android.com/ details?id=com.amazon.kindle

Blackberry
http://amazon.com/kindlebb

iPad and iPhone (universal app)
http://bit.ly/dY9Ooo

Windows XP, Vista or 7
http://amazon.com/gp/kindle/pc

Mac OS X
http://amazon.com/gp/kindle/ mac (or from the Mac App Store at *http://bit.ly/sdSdab*)

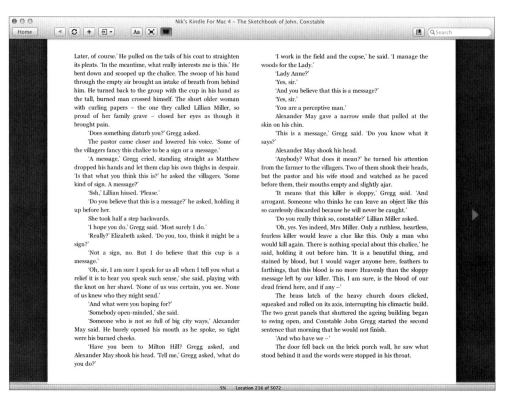

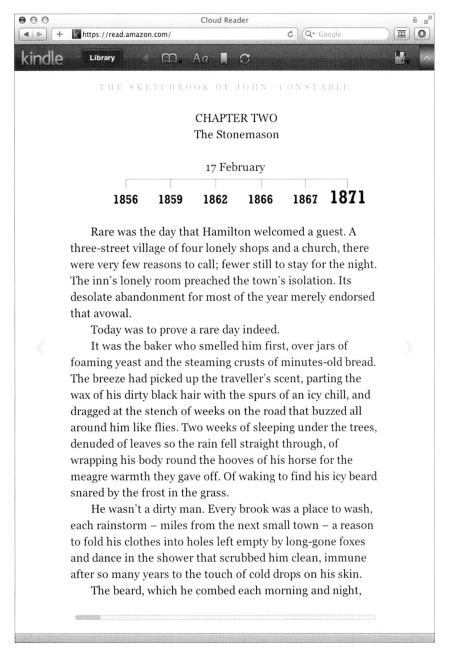

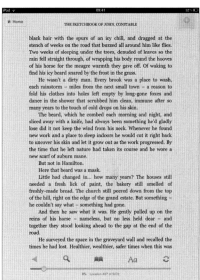

Above: The web-hosted Kindle reader gives you access to your complete library from anywhere in the world assuming you have a web connection. It also makes it easy to read books on any mobile device for which there isn't a dedicated Kindle app, or on which you'd rather not install one.

The Kindle iPhone (top) and iPad (bottom) apps replicate much of the reading experience, but miss the direct buying feature.

submitted them to the App Store for approval.

However, this wasn't an admission of defeat, for at the same time it started work on a browser-based reader, now hosted at *read. amazon.com* and built on HTML5.

This boasts many of the same features as the dedicated applications, and of course has a link to the Kindle section of Amazon's online store, effectively restoring the features of the native apps.

The browser reader obviously also works on regular desktop and laptop computers, but if you prefer to use a native application then check the box of links, far left,

and download the Kindle apps for Windows and Mac users.

Unfortunately Amazon doesn't provide a Linux version of its Kindle software, despite the Kindle hardware running Linux as their native operating systems. Linux users should therefore use WINE to run the Windows edition.

Organising books on an e-ink Kindle

Even the most basic Kindle can hold 1,400 books at a time. That's a lifetime's worth of reading for most people. To carry the same number of regular books would be impossible without the help of some kind of transport.

This is a boon for avid readers, but it can make finding each book somewhat tricky – unless you organise them into collections.

You can have several collections to handle different document types. So, you might want to create one for documents you've emailed to your Kindle, books you want to read, books you already have read, downloaded samples and so on.

To add a book to a collection, use the four-way controller to move down to it on the Home screen and press the right edge to call up the book options. The first of these is *Add to Collection...* Press the centre button to select it (*top right*).

We've already created one collection

our Kindle, called Read, where we file books we have finished reading. At present, as you can see from the image, it contains two books. It's already selected, so we only need press the centre button again to file our new book in this folder or, to put it elsewhere, move down one line to select *Create New Collection* and give the new folder a name.

By default your Kindle lists all of your books in order of use, with the most recently opened volume listed at the top of the Home screen.

In this state it will display all of your filed documents and books on the Home screen as well as inside their constituent collections (*grab 1, below*).

To change this, move the selection line up to the top of the screen and press right on the four-way controller, and change this to *Collections* (*grab 2*).

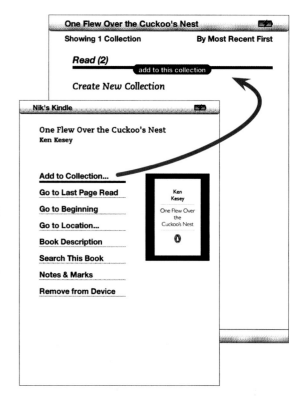

Your Home screen will now be reorganised, with the books you have filed in your collections (books we've finished reading in this case) hidden away inside your collections, making those you still have to open easier to find without all the clutter.

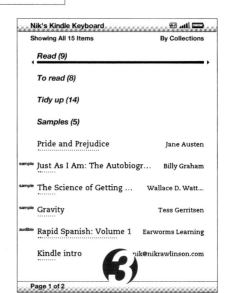

Lending books to friends and borrowing from a library

Kindle users in the US can loan ebooks to their Kindle-owning friends, but the feature isn't yet available elsewhere. Hopefully it's something Amazon will launch in the future, but in the meantime alternative ebook readers such as the Kobo and Sony Reader (*see pp16-17*) support library lending (*see below*) for users outside the US.

Lending for US readers

Amazon is encouraging more and more publishers to allow lending of their books. It's not a compulsory condition of being accepted into the Kindle store, but it is one of the criteria to which they must agree if they want to earn royalties of 70% on any of their titles.

You can loan a book by logging in to your Kindle dashboard or by pointing your browser at *Amazon. com* and clicking *Kindle | Manage Your Kindle* in the sidebar.

Here you'll see a list of all of the books bought through your account, complete with action buttons at the end of each line. Click the button and select *Loan this title* from the list of options.

You'll naturally need to tell Amazon who to lend the book to, by entering the recipient's name and email address plus, optionally, a message from yourself. They will then receive an email inviting them to borrow the book for 14 days, during which time it won't be available for you to read.

If they don't have a Kindle of their own they'll naturally have to download a Kindle application or use the online Cloud Reader at *read. amazon.com*.

Borrowing from libraries

Library lending is managed by the OverDrive system, an app for which – the OverDrive Media Console –

is available for a broad number of platforms, including the iPad and iPhone, Windows, Mac, Blackberry and Android devices. This gives readers all around the world access to their local library's stacks of ebooks and digital audio books.

Where the Kindle is concerned, though, library lending is still only available in the US at present, and while it is managed by OverDrive, the system retains many of the Kindle's best features (such as synchronising notes, highlights and page location across multiple devices). Your notes and highlights will remain tied to your Kindle account even after your permitted loan period of the book (which is determined by the rules of your local library) has expired.

This marks a big change for the OverDrive system, which previously made books available only in the ePub format, as used by Kobo, Sony Reader and iBooks on the iPad and iPhone, as it means that the company has been busily converting many of its titles to support the Kindle platform, which can't currently read ePub-formatted books.

OverDrive currently delivers books for 11,000 libraries and schools in the US, and 15,000 around the world. You can check whether your library is a member of its network at *search.overdrive.com*

Note that as well as requiring an Amazon account through which to download your borrowed book, you'll need to be a member of the library through which you want to borrow the title, as libraries are usually funded by public subscription through taxes.

Kindle
Hacks

I s
1/
fro
re
ab
fo
m
w

c
S
s
r

the last afternoon of Before constructing a
0-scale replica of the Empire State Building
oxes of adult diapers. It was a thing of beauty,
spanning five feet at its base and towering
the cosmetics aisle, with jumbos for the
tion, lites for the observation deck, and
lously stacked trial sizes for its iconic spire. It
most perfect, minus one crucial detail.
u used Neverleak," Shelley said, eyeing my
manship with a skeptical frown. "The sale's on
Tite." Shelley was the store manager, and her
ed shoulders and dour expression were as
a part of her uniform as the blue polo shirts
l had to wear.
thought you said Neverleak," I said, because
ad.
tay-Tite," she insisted, shaking her head
etfully, as if my tower were a crippled racehorse
she the bearer of the pearl-handled pistol. There
a brief but awkward silence in which she
inued to shake her head and shift her eyes from
to the tower and back to me again. I stared
kly at her, as if completely failing to grasp what
was passive-aggressively implying.
"Ohhhhhh," I said finally. "You mean you want

52%

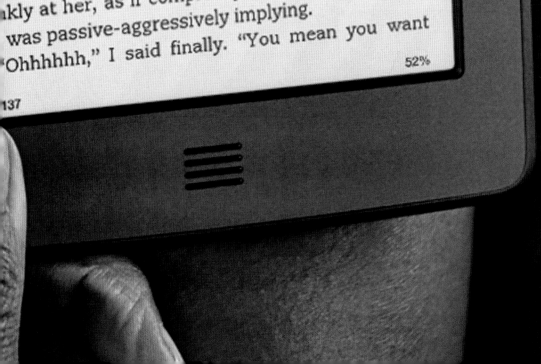

Publish your own Kindle book

Now that you've got to grips with downloading books and reading them on your Kindle, it's time to consider taking things further.

Thanks to the Kindle's (and Amazon's) organised, integrated, end-to-end distribution method that lets readers buy books directly on their devices, you can now publish your own material directly to your audience without following the usual route of finding an agent to represent you to the publishing industry and negotiate deals on your behalf. They might not like it, but at least you have less red tape to snip.

Clearly this means that you'll have to do more of the work yourself – and all of the promotion of your work, but as the person who understands what you have written better than anyone else, it makes sense for you to take on this role in the first place. Just prepare yourself for the fact that it means you may have less time to get on with writing

the second and third books in your (hopefully) best-selling saga.

Over the following ten pages we'll walk you through the steps involved in putting together your first Kindle book and selling it through Amazon's online store.

Learning from the pros

Barry Eisler landed himself a $500,000 publishing deal. He knew right away what he should do: he talked it over with his family, then turned it down.

Eisler isn't alone in turning his back on traditional publishing. A New York Times bestselling author, he's set himself up as a self publisher, convinced by a growing body of evidence that he'd earn more that way than any established imprint could pay him.

Eisler, like fellow author Joe Konrath, sees publishers' relevance diminishing in a rapidly-changing

industry. 'We're the writers. We provide the content that is printed and distributed,' Konrath wrote in response to Eisler's comments. 'For hundreds of years, writers couldn't reach readers without publishers. We needed them. Now, suddenly, we don't. But publishers don't seem to be taking this Very Important Fact into account.'

The rise of ebooks, the US sales of which overtook paperbacks as far back as February 2011, is putting the old-school publishers out of business – and their marketing departments, agents, and even bricks-and-mortar bookshops along with them – while ereaders like the Kindle and iPad are helping even novice authors find an audience, and make real money from writing.

Bypassing the print publishing cycle should lead not only to lower prices for the reader thanks to an increased level of competition between micro-publishers and a reduction in their overall costs (as they don't need to invest in paper, ink and physically shipping books around the world), but also greater reader choice. For most people, their bestselling, groundbreaking first novel remains unwritten not because of the effort involved in getting the words on the page, but through lack of faith that those pages will ever be read. Imagine what might happen if publication were not a remote possibility, but a dead cert.

Left: Amazon's clearly organised distribution channel links its online store to your readers' Kindles, allowing you to sell your books to them directly.

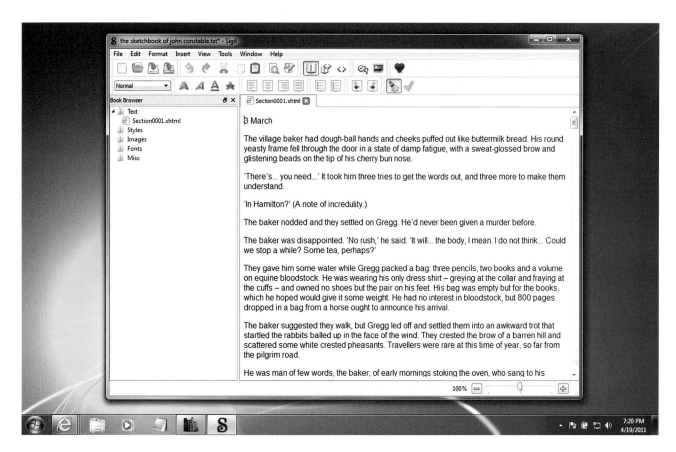

3 March

The village baker had dough-ball hands and cheeks puffed out like buttermilk bread. His round yeasty frame fell through the door in a state of damp fatigue, with a sweat-glossed brow and glistening beads on the tip of his cherry bun nose.

'There's... you need...' It took him three tries to get the words out, and three more to make them understand.

'In Hamilton?' (A note of incredulity.)

The baker nodded and they settled on Gregg. He'd never been given a murder before.

The baker was disappointed. 'No rush,' he said. 'It will... the body, I mean. I do not think... Could we stop a while? Some tea, perhaps?'

They gave him some water while Gregg packed a bag: three pencils, two books and a volume on equine bloodstock. He was wearing his only dress shirt – greying at the collar and fraying at the cuffs – and owned no shoes but the pair on his feet. His bag was empty but for the books, which he hoped would give it some weight. He had no interest in bloodstock, but 800 pages dropped in a bag from a horse ought to announce his arrival.

The baker suggested they walk, but Gregg led off and settled them into an awkward trot that startled the rabbits balled up in the face of the wind. They crested the brow of a barren hill and scattered some white crested pheasants. Travellers were rare at this time of year, so far from the pilgrim road.

He was man of few words, the baker, of early mornings stoking the oven, who sang to his

Signing a publishing contract is certainly something to celebrate, as it always has been, but it's no guarantee of success. Publishers make mistakes, just like the rest of us, pulping the 'next big thing' when it fails to find an audience, and passing up the chance to publish a blockbuster without ever seeing its brilliance.

The publishing world it littered with stories of successful authors who were turned down time and time again when they were just starting out, failing to get overworked, time-short publishers to show some interest in their work. JK Rowling and Stephen King, both household names with millions of book sales behind them, went through the process of sending samples of their work to leading agents and publishing houses, only to receive a rejection slip in return.

Remember, though, that success comes through actually selling books, not simply through having a Penguin embossed on your cover.

So, the more you sell, the greater your success, but how do you sell without a publisher? It isn't easy in print. The biggest sellers in any bookshop are stacked on the tables inside the door. Without a spot on the table, your chance of success is greatly diminished, but landing one is expensive.

That's where publishers are of greatest help to the first-time author. Bookshops can't afford to take a risk any more than a publisher can, and so often they will only stack books on these tables that have been heavily promoted in the press and already proved themselves to be likely sellers, either because they have been written by well-known and successful names, or because the publisher has committed a significant budget to promoting the title. Without a publisher you won't be able to afford to compete with them, and so the shop-front table is almost certainly out of your reach. So, too, are the readers those tables attract.

Above: Importing your raw text into Sigil is the first step in converting your document into a properly organised, sellable Kindle book.

There are no tables with eBooks. Publish on Kindle and you'll be given the same virtual shelf space as Dan Brown, and probably earn better royalties. Most mainstream authors receive considerably less than 15% of the cover price for each book sold, but you'll earn up to 70% without any ongoing costs.

You'll also receive your payments sooner. Each of your sales is electronic, so it can be accurately registered right away. Although readers who buy a Kindle book by accident can return it for a refund if they haven't started reading it, the majority of your sales should progress to completion. Amazon will record the royalty against your account and, a few weeks later, you'll receive a cheque or bank transfer, depending on what you've selected, in exchange for your sales.

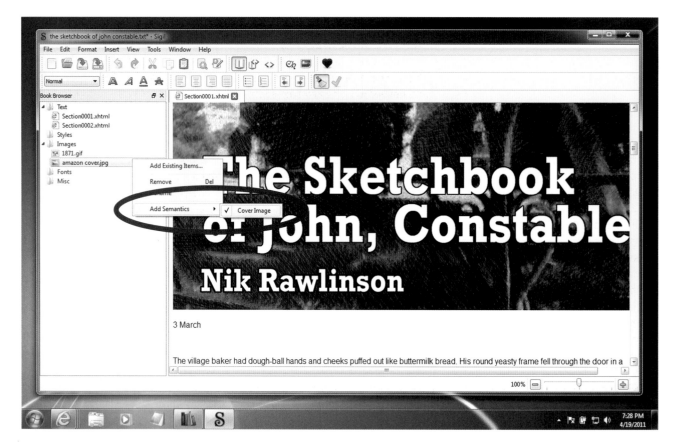

Above: Import your chosen image and then use the Add Semantics option on the formatting fly-out menu to mark it as your cover.

Compare that to the world of tradtional publishing. It can easily take a year or more for a printed book to find an agent, several months for the agent to sell it, and a year to a year and a half for your publisher to edit, print and market it in line with their leisurely schedules. Your royalties will likely be paid every six to 12 months, so your chance of earning anything within three years of typing The End are very slim indeed. Can you afford to wait that long when you have other books waiting to be written?

Save yourself the frustration, sidestep the traditional publishing route as we'll show you here, and you can be selling your book by next weekend. You'll have a three-year head start on your print-based rivals in which to start writing a sequel and beyond.

Formatting your book for Kindle

In the steps that follow we'll be using Sigil to format our book. Free to download from *code.google. com/p/sigil*, it's a cross-platform ebook editor that uses ePub as its native format. There are other platform-specific options, such as the excellent Scrivener on the Mac (at the time of writing Scrivener for Windows lacks e-book export options) but the following steps should work for both Mac and PC.

Here we'll be working through the formatting of a genuine published Kindle book, *The Sketchbook of John, Constable*. Written by the author of this MagBook, and published in the name of research, *The Sketchbook of John, Constable* proves how quick, simple and rewarding publishing your own ebook can be.

If your book is a plain text file then you have a head start, as you can open it directly inside Sigil. However, if you wrote it using Word,

you'll need to convert it first. From Word, pick *File | Save As...* and choose '*Web Page, Filtered*' as the format. Open the result in Sigil (*see the grab on p.47*).

Just like web pages, ePub files are highly structured, with their contents described in underlying code and arranged in a particular order so that, whatever the e-reader opens, the file will know exactly how to render the contents. Most e-readers, including the iBooks software that is free to download for use on the iPad, iPhone and iPod touch, use the ePub format, and although Amazon hinted that it may also allow this format in addition to its native book format in the latest release of Kindles, that hasn't happened. What we must do, therefore, is create Kindle-specific books if we want to sell them through Amazon's online store.

Our first job is to add the cover. Position your cursor at the very start of the text and press *ctrl-shift-i* (*command-shift-i* on the Mac) to open the image browser. Choose the picture you want to use and it will be added to the Images folder in the Sigil sidebar. At the moment it's nothing more than a floating asset in your raw ePub file and won't ever appear in the finished book until you tell the e-reader how to use it. We do this using 'semantics', which as the name suggests is merely a signpost describing what the image is and how it should be used, just as we'll later go on to define different text types.

To mark out this image as the cover, right click its entry in the sidebar (command-click on the Mac) and choose *Add Semantics | Cover Image* (*see the grab on p48*).

Images that you want to embed within the text are imported in exactly the same way, but without being marked for use as the cover. In this book, *The Sketchbook of John, Constable*, we're using a graphic timeline at the start of each chapter that would be impossible to render accurately using text. You

Kindle considerations

The e-ink Kindle's screen isn't colour, and neither will it be any time soon. Speaking to shareholders in May 2010, Amazon CEO Jeff Bezos said that the colour units it had in its labs were 'not ready for prime-time production'. For the moment, then, design two covers for your book – one colour version to display on Amazon's site, and a higher contrast, sharper monochrome edition to embed within the book. Make the Kindle edition 960 by 1280 pixels and it'll exactly fit the screen.

You can't lay out your ebook with the precision of a printed magazine. Your readers can choose their own font face and size, so aim for the lowest common denominator to guarantee the broadest compatibility: flowing text in a single column. Embed images within the flow of

the text rather than floating them to one side, as without knowing the dimensions of the screen in use you can't accurately predict how they will interact with the text.

Complex formatting, such as the timeline at the start of each chapter in *The Sketchbook of John, Constable*, should be created as a flat graphic to ensure they render accurately. Avoid trying to match any particular font. Kindle's default font is Caecilia, of which you can buy a single cut for as little as £25 (*http://bit.ly/e2Qmmg*), but how do you know your readers haven't switched to the sans-serif or condensed fonts, and they aren't reading it on a mobile device? Instead, choose the best font for the job, regardless of the surrounding text.

can see what this looks like in the image below. Although it appears large, the Kindle will automatically resize it to fit within the bounds of the screen when it appears in your finished book.

At this early stage, your book is a fairly unmanageable tract – just a long stretch of unformatted

text – that needs to be split into chapters. Position your cursor at the very start of chapter one, immediately after the cover image, and press *ctrl-return* (*command-return* on the Mac) to insert a chapter break. Do the same at the start of chapter two. You will now have three files in the sidebar's Text folder with consecutive numbers. *Section0001.xhtml* is your cover, *Section0002.xhtml* is chapter one and *Section0003.xhtml* is the rest of your book, which still needs to be further broken down. Continue working through the text, inserting a break before each chapter to create new files in the sidebar until you come to the end of the text (*see left*).

If you want to include a table of contents in your book, use the style

Left: Work your way through your book, inserting breaks within the text to denote the start of each chapter. Each one will appear as a notch on the Kindle progress bar.

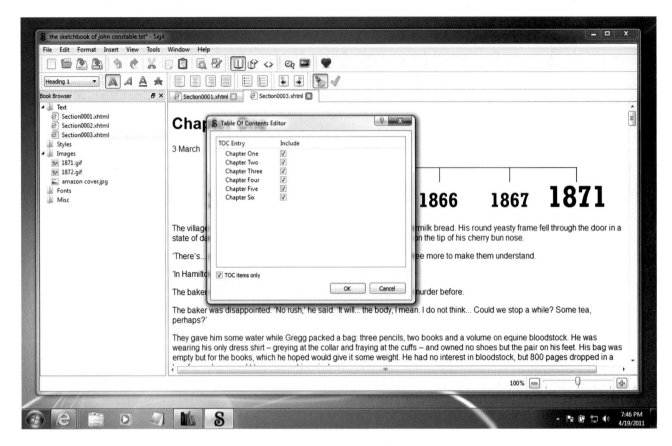

menu on the left of the toolbar as you create your chapters to mark each title as a Heading. There are six heading styles to choose from, with *Heading 1* uppermost in the hierarchy. Press F7 to open the table of contents editor and uncheck any headings that you don't want to include in the table when you compile your book (*see above*).

Your book is progressing well. You have split up your text into chapter sections and given each one a title so that it's easy to identify on the screen and can be navigated either by clicking the headings in the table of contents, or by using the Kindle's four-way rocker

button, clicking left or right to jump backwards or forwards through the novel. You now need to think about how your book is going to be filed and sold online by adding all of the necessary author and title data that will identify it.

Do this by pressing F8 to open the metadata editor and then enter, at the very least, the title of your

book and the author's name so that it can be accurately catalogued by online stores. To add further details like the imprint, ISBN, rights and so on, click More and use the Add Basic and Add Adv. buttons to add both common and more esoteric metadata. The more you add, the more accurately your book will be catalogued (*see below*).

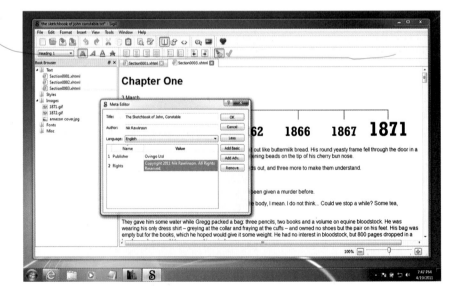

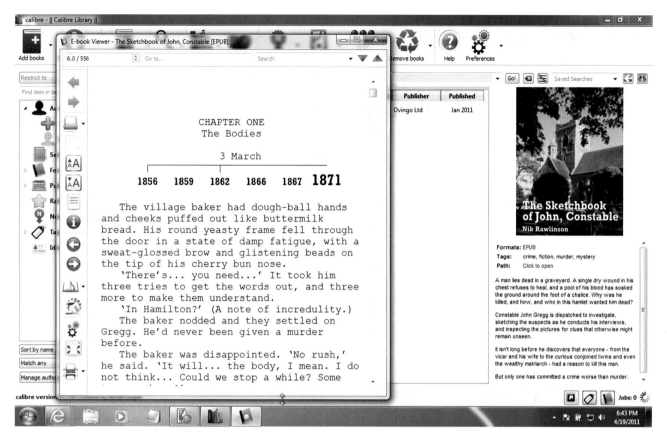

When you've finished formatting your book, save it in Sigil's native ePub format. This is the format used by the majority of ebook readers, including iBooks on the iPad and iPhone, but not Kindle or Kindle apps, which use a modified version of Mobipocket. While the Kindle Direct Publishing process (*see Publish and Be Damned*) will handle the conversion, for the best and most predictable results you should perform the conversion yourself and test your book locally on your own Kindle.

We'll do this using Calibre, an open source ebook library tool that's free to download from *calibre-ebook.com*. When you first install it you'll have to tell it where to file your library, but beyond that all management tasks, including conversions between different book formats, are conducted through the graphical user interface.

You can add whole books to your Calibre library in a number of ways, from the simple step of entering

an ISBN (*see the Beyond Kindle boxed text, p.55*) for which it will retrieve the cover art and metadata, to importing a complete book file for reading and manipulation. We need the latter, so click Add Books and navigate to your formatted epub document (*see above*).

Calibre copies the book to its library and uses the metadata you entered in Sigil to catalogue it.

To check that it has accurately imported your book, double-click its cover in the library to preview the contents. You should be able to click to the start of each chapter in the table of contents, and click forwards and back through the pages using the purple arrows. If it works as you expect, you're ready to convert it to Kindle's native format.

Click *Convert Books*, and select Mobi as the output format from the pull-down menu at the top right of the conversion panel. The input format should already be set to ePub, our book's current format.

Click *Page Setup* to check that

Left: The Calibre ebook processing and management tool makes short work of converting your ePub-formatted publication into the Mobipocket format used by Amazon's Kindle products, apps and browser-based software.

Generic e-ink is selected as the output profile (e-ink is the screen technology used in most Kindle models). If it is, click *OK* to perform the conversion. From here on in everything is automated. The progress spinner at the bottom of the library window will show you it's working, but when it stops it won't be immediately obvious where it's put the completed document. To find it, select the book in the library and click the link beside Path in the book details pane.

Connect your Kindle to a free USB port on your computer and either drag the Mobipocket-formatted book to your device's Documents folder, or use the Send To Device button on the Calibre

CHAPTER ONE

The Bodies

3 March

1856   1859   1862   1866   1867   **1871**

The village baker had dough-ball hands and cheeks puffed out like buttermilk bread. His round yeasty frame fell through the door in a state of damp fatigue, with a sweat-glossed brow and glistening beads on the tip of his cherry bun nose.

'There's... you need...' It took him three tries to get the words out, and three more to make them understand.

'In Hamilton?' (A note of incredulity.)

1%

Left: After conversion to Mobipocket format our book is compatible with the Kindle. Copying it to our device lets us check that it looks like we want and that the contents, navigation and chapter headings work properly.

toolbar to upload it. You can then eject your Kindle in the usual way.

Your new book will appear at the top of the Kindle home screen. Open it in the usual way to check that it looks as you'd expect and that you're happy for it to be published on Amazon in this form. Check in particular that the table of contents is in tact (press *Menu | Go to... | table of contents*) and that clicking the links there takes you to the relevant points in the book. Check also that your chapter markers are in place. These are the notches cut into the progress bar at the foot of the reading display. Using the left- and right-hand edges of the four-

way controller skips you backwards and forwards a chapter at a time, rather than moving page by page. (*see grab, above*).

If it all works as it should, you're ready to take the final step and publish your book on Amazon.

Publish and be damned

Log in to the Kindle Direct Publishing dashboard at *http://kdp.amazon.com* using your regular Amazon account details. Before you can sell books through the online store you'll need to agree to Amazon's terms and conditions. You will also see a warning in the

top corner of the Dashboard screens informing you that your account information is incomplete. Click it and enter your address and how you'd like to be paid. You'll have to wait until you hit £100 of sales if you want to be paid by cheque, but if you're happy to accept an electronic funds transfer (EFT) straight into your bank account, Amazon will make a payment for every £10 earned. You'll need to choose cheque or EFT for each of the territories in which Amazon sells electronic books, but bear in mind that foreign sales will be paid into your account in that country's local currency, for which your bank may charge a handling fee.

Once you have agreed to the terms and conditions and entered your address and account details you can start the publishing process.

Return to your bookshelf and click *Add a new title*. Work your way through the publishing form, at the very least giving a title, language and author name, as well as a description of up to 4,000 characters. This is the blurb that appears on the book's listings page, both on the Amazon web pages and the store pages accessed directly through the Kindle, so think carefully about what you write here and come up with something that showcases your work.

Amazon needs to know where to file your book in its catalogue by specifying the categories under which it should be filed. You'll need to select the two most relevant options, and at the same time can optionally type in your own descriptive tags to help improve its search performance (*see top right*).

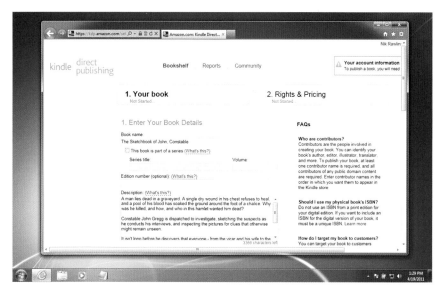

Above: Work your way through the publishing screens to write an enticing description of your book and add metadata to help file it.

Amazon sells both public domain books and those for which copyright still applies, and requires all publishers to specify into which camp their book falls. Public domain books can still be charged for, even if you haven't contributed to them yourself, but they only ever attract royalties of 35%.

It's up to you whether or not you upload a cover image, but we'd strongly recommend it. If you don't, Amazon will use a flat placeholder that will do little to sell your work. Remember, the key thing to keep in mind when working your way through these screens is that everything you do should help to entice readers and generate more sales – and thus more revenue – for you. A well-designed cover image is a key part of this.

Ensure that whatever image you choose it is RGB, rather than CMYK, at least 500 pixels wide and no more than 1,280 pixels tall. If your background is white, add a 3-pixel

Right: Decide how much you want to charge for your book, bearing in mind that this will affect the level of royalties you will receive.

thick grey border to help it stand out on the Amazon listing pages. This cover image isn't the same as the one that forms part of your book: that's embedded within the Kindle file itself, so can be optimised for the Kindle screen.

Still with us? Good. You're almost there.

Finally, you need to decide whether you want to enable Digital Rights Management (DRM) and then upload your actual book file.

Digital Rights Management is a way in which your book can be encoded such that it can't be passed on from one reader to another, except in line with Amazon's usual rules about loaning books for a

short, specified period. You can't change your mind on the DRM issue once you've published your book, so think very carefully whether you're happy for people to share your work without making any further payments to yourself before going beyond this point.

Amazon will check your uploaded file and, assuming it meets its requirements, will let you complete the publishing process. This involves choosing the territories in which the book should be sold and what royalties you'd like to earn. The standard share is 35% of the cover price, but if price your book between £1.49 and £6.99 and enable lending you can hike it to a very generous 70% in the UK and US (*see below*).

Think back to what we said earlier here: by following the traditional publishing route you would be lucky to earn royalties of around 15% on net receipts – ie wholesale prices, after discounts of 50% or more have been given to

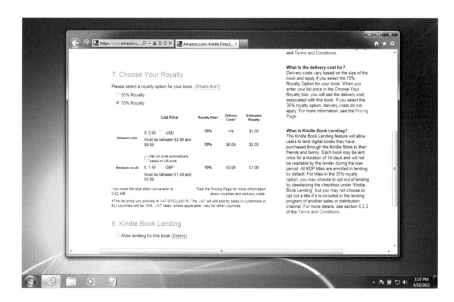

retailers as an inducement to take your book. On a £7.99 / $7.99 book, then, even if you swing royalties of 15%, you might earn 59p / 59c. From this, your agent would also take a cut of 10% to 15%.

Sell your book for £1.99 / $1.99 on Kindle, on the other hand, and you can opt for 70% royalties, which will earn you £1.39 / $1.39 per copy while still significantly undercutting the mainstream publishers and increasing your chance of a sale. Reduce your price yet further to the lowest level at which you'd qualify for 70% royalties, and you'd still

Below: At the end of our publishing and approval process our book is online and ready for download.

earn over £1 / $1 for each copy sold, while encouraging readers to buy a copy of your book because it is such a bargain when compared to mainstream novelists' work.

Don't believe us? There's plenty of evidence that it works.

Novelist Joe Konrath was selling his book, The List, for $2.99. Through the first two weeks of February 2011 it sold an average of 43 copies a day, each of which earned him royalties of 70%, pulling in $87 daily. On the 15th of the month, he dropped the price to just 99 cents – a level that is eligible for royalties of only 35% – and sales increased massively. It went from being the 1078th best-selling charged-for book in the Kindle Store

to 78th. Daily sales increased to 533 copies, and although the amount of money earned by each one fell from $2.03 to just 35 cents, his average daily earnings now stood at $187. Dropping the price – and the royalties – has more than paid for itself in his case.

UK ebook publishers should bear in mind when setting your pricing that Customs and Excise counts ebooks as 'services' (the service being the act of serving the download), and as services attract VAT this will also apply to your ebook. Amazon adds this to your asking price using the rate charged in Luxembourg at the time of purchase. At the time of writing this stands at 15%, so if you're looking to

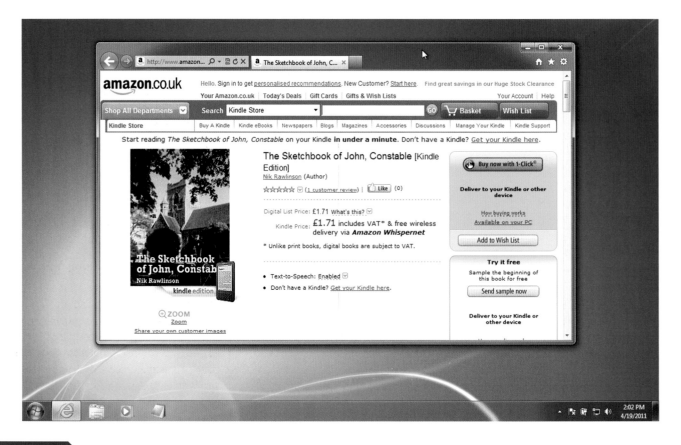

Beyond Kindle

Amazon is the most accessible market for first-time authors, but it's not the only one. Apple's iBookstore signed up 2,500 publishers in its first nine months and sold over 100 million books. Waterstones in the UK sells ebooks for the Sony Reader and in the US Barnes & Noble has its own Nook device. Beyond these there are countless independent outlets targeting third-party devices.

Unless you've registered with the US tax system, the easiest way to sell through each of them is to use an approved aggregator such as *lulu.com*. As well as publishing single-copy print editions of user-uploaded books, Lulu will push content into the iBookstore and other ebook outlets by assigning your novel a free ISBN (International Standard Book Number).

This is a stock control code that uniquely identifies every published book to simplify the cataloguing and ordering process. The numbers are assigned in batches to registered publishers by national agencies of the International Standard Book Numbering Convention. The UK agency is Nielsen Book (*www.isbn.nielsenbook.co.uk*).

To publish books under your own imprint through Lulu you must register with your local ISBN agency and buy a batch of numbers. In the UK it costs £118.68 (inc. VAT) for your first 10 ISBNs. Each subsequent batch of 10 ISBNs cost £66.36, with discounts open to more prolific publishers. Each ISBN can be used only once, and on one format, so you can't use the same ISBN on both the ePub and Kindle versions of your book.

are already familiar with this convention from its widespread use in printed books.

If you do need to include images then you should be sure to use your image editor's save for web function to intelligently compress those you do use and minimise your charges. Careful, judicious use of this tool often allows you to significantly reduce the file size of an image without having any visible detrimental effect on its appearance. This is because the human eye is better at detecting interference in parts of an image demonstrating significant change, and so it can safely reduce the amount of information used to describe the make-up of flatter, simpler areas. Throwing away this redundant data will significantly reduce your delivery bills and increase your overall income.

Because of the approval process involved, it usually takes Amazon two working days to publish an English language book, after which the Dashboard's Reports section will show your earnings week by week. It takes longer to publish in foreign languages, so don't leave things until the last moment. If you are planning on publishing to meet a particular deadline plan ahead, and be prepared to have your book on the digital shelves a little earlier than required so that you don't risk missing out on potential sales.

Following the simple processes described over the last couple of pages, you can not only get your much treasured piece of literature into the public arena, but you'll also have great fun doing it and, you never know, might make some cash.

hit the magical 99p price point you'll actually have to price your book at just 86p. From this you'll earn 30p per copy. At this price you'll either need to sell a lot of copies to make it worth your while, or be writing and publishing books for fun and satisfaction.

Amazon will will 'deliver' your book electronically for free if you opt for 35% royalties, but if you choose 70% it will charge you 10p (UK) or 15 cents (US and Canada) per megabyte to send it to your readers. The size of the book is calculated when you upload it, and the charge worked out pro-rata to the nearest kilobyte. So, a book that weighs in at 200KB would cost 2p or 3 cents to deliver, depending on territory, which would be deducted from your royalties.

Although words and numbers don't consume a great deal of either storage space or bandwidth when delivered, images are considerably more space-hungry, which is why comparatively few highly illustrative books have traditionally been converted for sale through the Kindle store. This is because they must each be encoded and embedded within the book, and is the reason why the timeline graphics that we used when formatting *The Sketchbook of John, Constable*, were kept very simple and rendered in just one colour.

It is therefore worth thinking very carefully before including purely decorative images in your book – even as markers to appear at the end of a chapter of between sections. Often these can be replaced by regular characters which, however ornate they appear to be, would each only count as a single letter and so dramatically reduce the cost of delivering your book. Further, it is often better to simply leave a single blank line between sections within a chapter as readers

Hidden Kindle features

Thought your Kindle was just an ebook reader? Think again. Amazon has built in several hidden features, which are easily uncovered with a little smart web searching.

These tips rely on having a keyboard, so work on most Kindle 2, Kindle DX and Kindle Keyboard models.

Kindle picture viewer

Your Kindle may only have a monochrome screen, but that doesn't stop publishers putting images in their books – or, indeed, on their covers – so why shouldn't you also take advantage of its ability to render a good pictures?

Connect your Kindle to your PC or Mac and open its internal storage. Here you should find four folders: audible, documents, music and pictures. If any of them are missing you can create them.

Optimise your pictures for display on the Kindle's monochrome screen to reduce their file sizes. Optionally convert them to greyscale, and if possible reduce the image size so that it is no more than 900 in any direction, vertically or horizontally. Although your Kindle will accept larger images and shrink them down to fit on the screen, you're just wasting space on your device as it'll have to throw away a lot of the excess data.

Now create a folder inside pictures to hold your new images. We've called ours 'holiday' (*right*) and dropped a number of our pictures into it.

Eject your Kindle and if the new folder doesn't appear on the Home screen press Alt and Z to refresh the listing. Select the new folder, which will appear in the list of books, and the first of your photos will load for your gallery.

Use the regular forward and backwards page turning buttons to move through the album, and press the Aa button to change the gallery options (*bottom*), choosing whether to show the whole of the image on screen or stretch it to fit the height or width, and whether you want to rotate your Kindle display, which works well with landscape shots (*bottom left*).

Nik's Kindle Keyboard

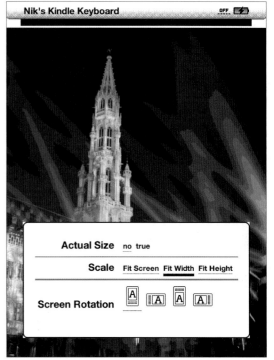

Nik's Kindle Keyboard

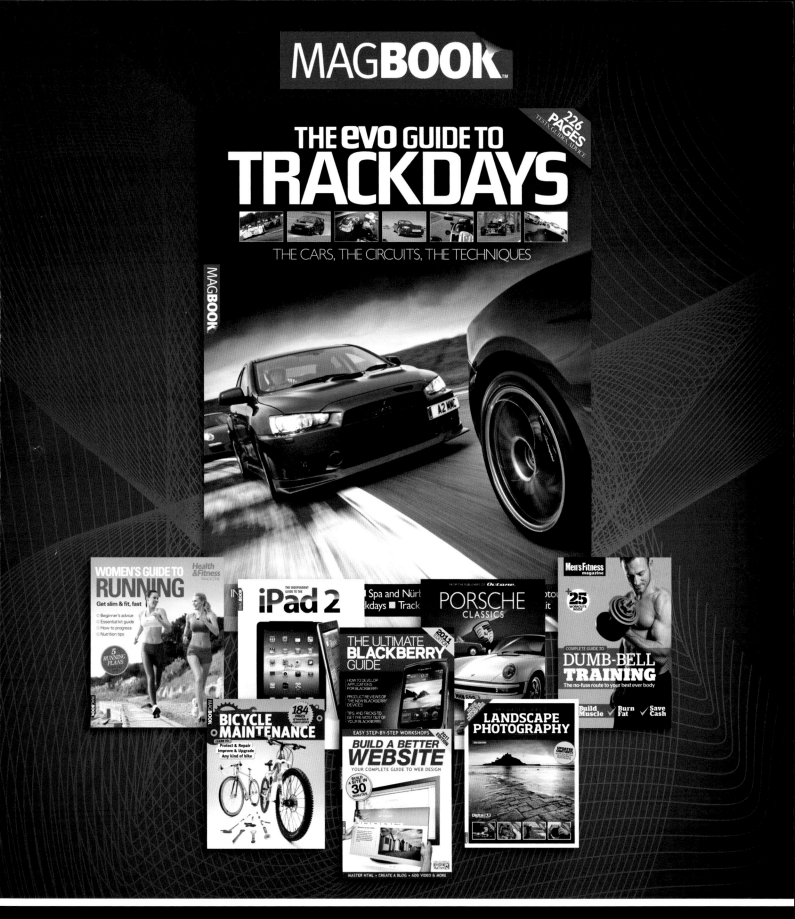

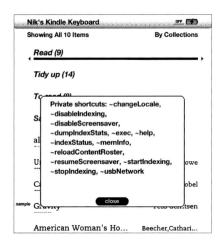

Music while you read

Who doesn't like to listen to music while they read a book? Kindle has this covered.

Connect your Kindle Keyboard to your Mac or PC, open its internal storage and drop a selection of MP3 tracks into the Music folder (you can create this folder if it doesn't exist).

Disconnect your Kindle and choose a book to read. To listen to your music in the background, hold Alt while pressing space; do the same to stop the music, and press Alt and F to skip to the next track.

Kindle calculator

The Kindle has a fully-fledged Linux operating system under its hood, which in places pokes out through the reading interface, allowing you to take advantage of some of its core features, including maths functions.

To use your Kindle as a calculator, return to the Home screen (this doesn't work from any

of the reading screens) and press any character on the keyboard to bring up the search box. Delete that character and replace it with your sum (see our Quick Tip on the facing page for a shortcut when entering numbers). When you have finished tapping in your sum, press the centre of the four-way controller to perform the search and see the result (*below left*).

You can perform some pretty advanced sums in this way, using braces to mark out parts of a sum that should be performed first, with the answer to that part used in the rest of the calculation, and the caret symbol (^) to mark powers. In this respect 100^2 would be equivalent to 100².

Kindle for geeks

Your Kindle isn't as simple as it looks. In reality, it keeps an eye on everything you do and notes it down in a log. For the truly technical who want to see what's been going on in the background, go to the Home screen and type *;debugOn* followed by return.

Now type *;dumpMessages* and again press return. Your Kindle will freeze for a few seconds as it retrieves all of the data, before dropping it into your list of books, ready for reading. For a full set of debug menu options, type *~help* and press return to call up a panel showing your options (*above*).

TEXT TO SPEECH

Too tired to keep reading but want to finish your book? Kindle Keyboard users can press *shift + SYM* to activate text to speech. The results are surprisingly good. Don't forget to plug in headphones if you don't want to disturb those around you on public transport.

Pressing the AA button when using text to speech doesn't open the regular font control panel, but launches speech controls (*below*), allowing you to change the speed at which the book is read out and what gender of voice to use.

In our experience, the male voice seems to give a smoother, less jumpy result, but slowing down the female voice improves it. Remember to set it back to default if you want to switch back to male.

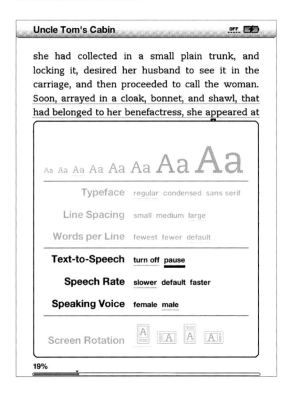

Find the mines!

OFF

Press the M key to mark/unmark mine
Press the R key to restart
Press the G key to play GoMoku

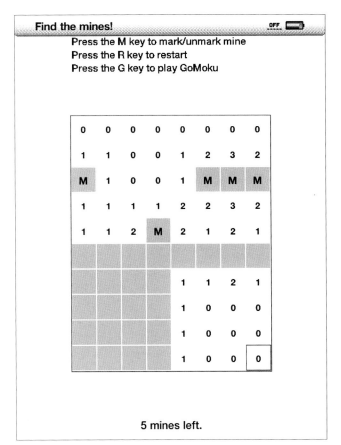

5 mines left.

Get five in a row!

OFF

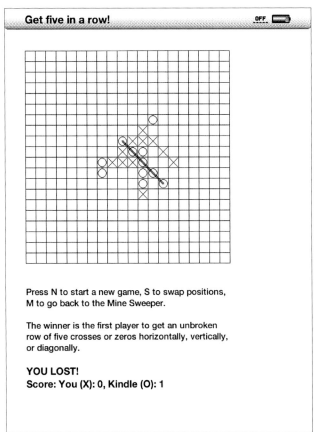

Press N to start a new game, S to swap positions, M to go back to the Mine Sweeper.

The winner is the first player to get an unbroken row of five crosses or zeros horizontally, vertically, or diagonally.

YOU LOST!
Score: You (X): 0, Kindle (O): 1

Kindle Games

If you're buying a Kindle to play games, then invest in a Kindle Fire, which will open up access to the Amazon Appstore from which you can download a wide variety of top games, including Words With Friends and Angry Birds.

If you have a Kindle 2 or Kindle Keyboard, however, and want a quick game or two to pass the time while you're waiting for an appointment, you'll find two hidden in the operating system.

Return to the Home screen and press *Shift-Alt-M* to switch to Mine Sweeper. Windows users will remember this game from their desktop computer, but for anyone who hasn't played it, your Kindle has hidden 10 sea mines in an ocean that is eight squares wide and 10 deep. Your task is to find them all without hitting any of them. Use the four-way controller to move your position around the board and press

the central button to uncover the highlighted square. Kindle gives you some help by showing how many mines border any particular square to help you avoid a nasty surprise.

If you turn up a square bordered by no mines, Mine Sweeper will reveal a whole block of empty squares until it reaches a strip that does border a mine.

Once you've mastered Mine Sweeper, try your hand at GoMoku, accessed from the same shortcut.

This is like Connect 4 on a grand scale. Your task is to line up five of your 'X' characters in a row, horizontally, vertically or diagonally. Meanwhile, your Kindle will be trying to do the same thing while also blocking you as you get closer to your goal. You therefore need to keep an eye on what it's doing, as if it achieves five in a row before you, you've lost.

To exit the games, press the Home button to return to your list of books.

QUICK TIP

The accepted method of entering numbers is to switch to the *SYM*bol keyboard and use the four-way controller to hunt and peck the on-screen characters to enter each one (*below*). This is effective, but time consuming. If you only want to enter numbers, save time by instead holding *Alt* while pressing the top row of letter keys. Q to O give you the numbers 1 to 9, while P will give you a zero.

How to manage your Kindle remotely

Although the Kindle has all the tools you need to manage it pre-installed, it's often faster – and more convenient – to manage it remotely. This allows you to use a full-sized keyboard, mouse, and browser to perform what might otherwise be fiddly tasks, should you find yourself restricted to using the Kindle's physical or on-screen keyboard and its four way pointer.

We have already seen how easy it is to buy books though a regular browser and send them to your Kindle; here we'll take a closer look at the other actions you can perform through the browser using the Kindle dashboard, through which Amazon lets you access each of your registered Kindle devices. Get started by picking *Kindle | Manage Your Kindle* from the sidebar. If you haven't recently entered your password you'll need to add it on the next screen to progress any further.

Although you'll spend most of your time reading books on your Kindle, it's also capable of downloading newspapers and magazines and subscribing to blogs, with daily, weekly or monthly updates to each one automatically downloaded to your device as a subscription.

Authorising document uploads

One of the simplest ways to get new content onto your Kindle, other than books bought from Amazon, is to email it to the address associated with each device, as displayed on the top line of its section on the dashboard. To prevent your Kindle being spammed, click *Personal Document Settings* and

Navigate the Kindle dashboard

Transfer documents by emailing them to this address. You need a different address for each device.

Use this menu to switch between the different media types registered to your Kindle account.

Want to sell or give away your Kindle? Be sure to use the Deregister option here to unlink it from your account. You can also deregister Kindle applications using the table below.

Turn of synchronisation if you and a friend are reading the same book, bought on the same account, on different Kindles to prevent one from affecting the other's page position.

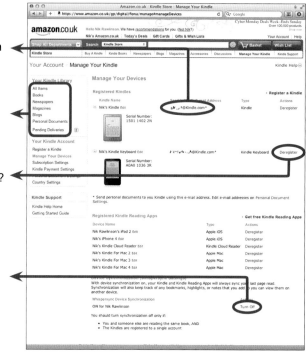

first choose the email addresses at which you want each Kindle to receive incoming documents, and then scroll down to the *Approved Personal Document E-mail List* section and specify which addresses can send you documents.

You can store up to 5GB of documents in your online Kindle library, as well as on your Kindle itself. This is turned on by default, but you can disable it by clicking Edit in the *Personal Document Archiving* section.

Changing your home store

If you bought your Kindle directly from Amazon it will be registered to the national store through which you bought it. This makes it easy to start buying and enjoying content

right away. If for any reason you need to change to an alternative national store, click *Country Settings*, followed by the *Learn More* link (clicking the *Change* link at the end of the current country line only lets you update your address).

UK customers can't simply go shopping in the US store (and vice versa) as though they were tourists. Instead you must transfer your account by clicking *Learn about transferring your Kindle account to Amazon.com* (or *.co.uk*) and authorising the transfer.

This will switch all of your existing purchases to your new chosen Amazon country and charge you in the new local currency for future purchases. Depending on your bank you may incur currency conversion fees or commission.

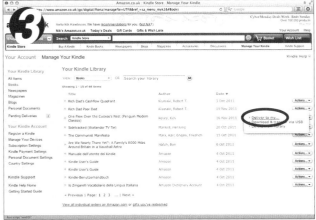

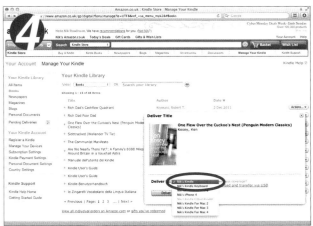

How to manage your Kindle library through a browser

Skill level
Beginner – a simple task that everyone can complete

Time required
Up to 30 minutes, depending on the amount of management involved

Equipment required
PC or Mac, with a browser

1. Log in to your account through your home country's Amazon homepage and select *Kindle | Manage Your Kindle* from the Departments panel on the left hand side of the page. By default this calls up a list of books you've bought on any one of your Kindles or Kindle apps installed on a third-party device. You can switch to other media types by clicking them in the sidebar, and expand the details of each bought item by clicking the '+' beside its name. Expand the details of one of your books now to start managing your Kindle.

2. Click *View Product Page* to open the book's original location in Amazon's catalogue, or *Order Details* to view full details of your order, including how much you paid, when you bought it and Amazon's order reference. You can also print an order summary here if you bought the book for business purposes and need a proof of purchase.

3. Return to the list of products you've downloaded to perform the full set of management tasks. Click the *Actions...* button to call up a menu that allows you to either delete the book from your library or send it to other Kindle devices. Don't delete a book without due care, as if you later want to read it again you'll have to purchase a new copy.

4. Choose *Deliver to my...* and then select the device you'd like to send it to using Amazon's Whispernet network over either 3G or wifi, depending on your model. All of your hardware Kindles and any registered Kindle apps will already be listed here so all you need do is choose one.

Note that even if you choose to transfer the book using USB you will still need to specify its destination so that Amazon can apply the necessary Digital Rights Management measures to ensure that the book isn't passed on.

How to wirelessly send documents to your Kindle

The Kindle is, at heart, a book reader. However, books can come in a wide variety of formats. Most of us think of a traditional book as a bound collection of pages, which in Kindle format has been transformed into a flowing text file with changeable font faces, text sizes and line spacing.

However, the Kindle can also handle a wide range of other document types, including PDF, plain text, Word .doc and .docx, Jpeg, Gif, PNG, BMP and others.

As we have already pointed out, you can load documents onto your Kindle directly by connecting it using the bundled USB cable and dragging them onto the Kindle's internal storage using your Mac or PC's regular filesystem.

Transferring files wirelessly

However, every Kindle has a wifi connection, and many also feature 3G, so it makes sense to transfer your documents wirelessly and thus save yourself the task of connecting it to your computer.

Before doing so, you need to authorise your email addresses to send documents to your Kindle. This is an anti-spam measure that Amazon has implemented to prevent people from sending random documents to your Kindle device, using up your storage space and Amazon's network bandwidth.

To do this, click *Kindle | Manage Your Kindle | Personal Document Settings* and click the link to *Add a new approved email address*. Double-check before clicking Add Address, and then log out of your account.

Skill level	Beginner – a simple task that everyone can complete
Time required	Around five minutes
Equipment required	Any Kindle model, plus a computer with a live Internet connection and an email client

STEP BY STEP

1. Start by checking the email address to which you need to send your documents. This will have been set by Amazon and is based on your Amazon account name. Find it by pressing the Kindle menu button and then selecting Settings from the drop-down.

2. Navigate to the second page of the settings utility to find your address, which will take the form of *<username>@kindle.com*.

3. If you're not happy with your assigned address you can specify a new one through your Amazon account. Log in using a regular browser and click *Kindle | Manage Your Kindle | Personal Document Settings*. Here you'll find details of the email address assigned to each of your Kindles. To change one of them, click the Edit button at the end of its entry and enter a new username. You can't change the *@kindle.com* part of the address.

4. Start a new email using your regular email or webmail application, addressed to your Kindle's email address, and attach the file you want to convert and read on your device. You'll receive an email confirming the transfer and, if wireless or 3G is active on your device, the document will appear on your home screen automatically.

QUICK TIP

When your document arrives on your Kindle it'll be filed under your email address on the Kindle home screen.

At the same time, It'll be filed on Amazon's cloud storage servers so that you can access it again in the future. Every account includes 5GB of free cloud storage, so if you're getting close to your limit you'll want to delete your older documents. Log in through a browser and pick *Kindle | Manage Your Kindle | Personal Document Settings* to manipulate your documents through a regular browser and free up some space.

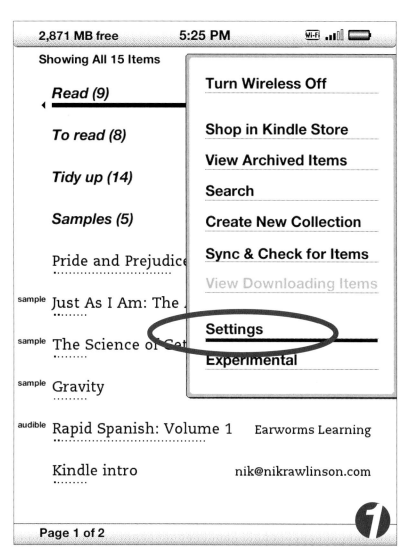

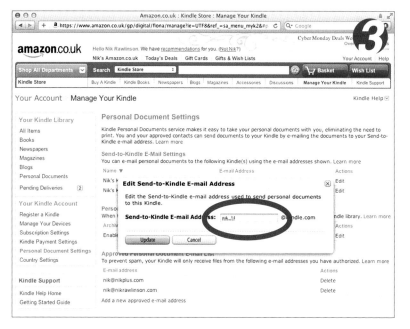

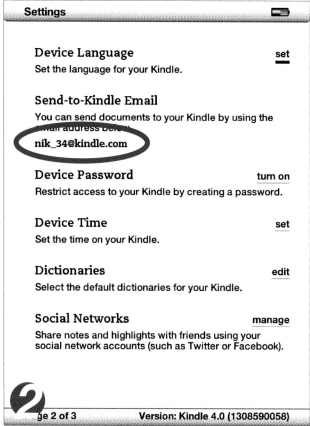

Set up your Kindle to work with Instapaper

Now that you know how to send documents to your Kindle, you can link it to an Instapaper account, allowing you to send it documents that you don't have time to read during regular browsing. Instapaper is a free service that allows you to mark web pages for reading later on using a button on your regular browser toolbar. Sign up at *instapaper.com*, and drag the toolbar button into your browser.

Follow the instructions here to tie your Inspapaper and Kindle accounts together, and whenever you mark a page you don't have time to read, it'll appear on your Kindle home screen within 24 hours.

QUICK TIP

Every time a new document is emailed to your Kindle, Amazon will send you an email to let you know that it's ready for reading. These are purely for your own information and so long as the documents are only coming from your authorised addresses they can be safely deleted or ignored.

Skill level	Intermediate
Time required	Around five minutes
Equipment required	Kindle, Kindle Touch or Kindle Keyboard, including previous generation devices; Free Inspapaper account

STEP BY STEP

1. Log in to your Inspapaper account using a regular web browser and visit *http://www.instapaper.com/user/kindle* to set up forwarding on your account. Start by checking the box to *Send my Unread articles to my Kindle automatically* and choose from the drop-down boxes whether you'd like them sending daily or weekly (in which case they'll be sent on Friday morning) and how many unread articles there should be in your reading queue to trigger a delivery. We have set ours to 1 new article and daily deliveries, so that any stories we mark for reading should reach our Kindle within 24 hours.

2. You now need to authorise Instapaper to load content onto your Kindle. This is a two stage process that takes place on both the Instapaper site and your Kindle dashboard. Start by entering your Kindle email address, copying it from your Kindle dashboard to the box on your Instapaper account. If you're happy to only have documents delivered over wifi select *@free.kindle.com* as the extension. If you have a 3G-enabled Kindle and would also like files to be delivered over the mobile network then leave it set to *@kindle.com*, although note that you will be charged a fee for delivery, depending on the size of the archive.

    Now head for your Kindle dashboard and add the Instapaper address shown in green to the list of approved email addresses so that Amazon doesn't automatically reject incoming archives as spam.

    Click *Add Address* on the Kindle dashboard and *Save changes* on the Instapaper site, then check that everything is working by clicking *Send now* on the Instapaper page to immediately send an archive of your currently-saved documents from Instapaper to your Kindle.

3. If your Kindle is switched on and has an active Internet connection you'll soon see an archive of your unread documents appear on the home screen. This will have the title *Instapaper* and, because you may receive several such archives before you have read them, will sport the current date as the author name.

4. By bundling all of your documents together, Instapaper has built a fully indexed collection. Skip to the table of contents for quick links to each one or use the right and left-hand edges of the four way controller to skip forwards and backwards to the start of each item. Use the regular page turning controls to read the individual screens inside each article as you would a normal book.

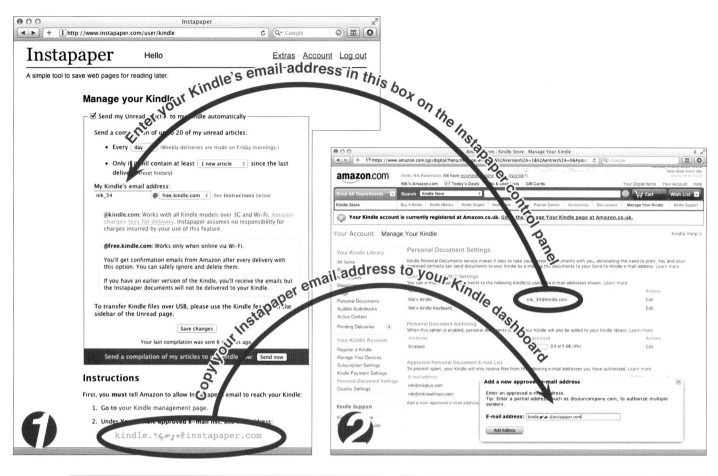

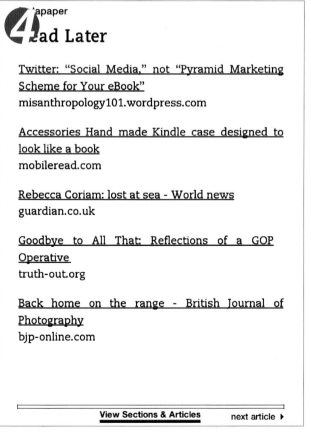

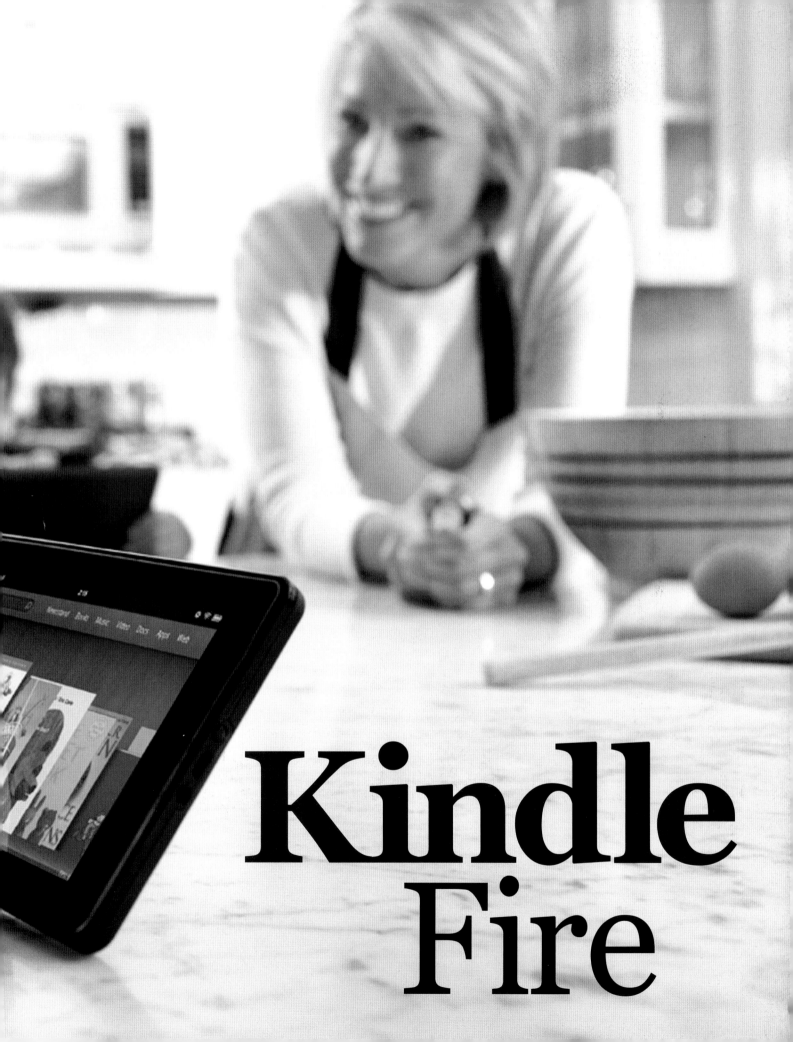

Kindle
Fire

Kindle Fire in depth

Kindle Fire is Amazon's most ambitious reading device to date. With a 7in colour back-lit LCD display it's a fully-fledged Android-based tablet computer, on which readers can install their own applications, as well as download books, videos and music from the Amazon online store. For anyone who wants to read magazines just as much as they do books, it's a great choice, allowing them to enjoy pages in rich colour, packed with graphics, original layouts and creative fonts.

Kindle Fire draws on each of Amazon's various businesses. It's a long time since the company was only a retailer of books; it now has an MP3 download store, a movie distribution service courtesy of LoveFilm and massive online storage resources built on the back of its own cloud computing platform. Each of these plays a part in making the Fire a success, feeding in up to date info and making it possible to store your own content online.

Amazon Appstore

The Appstore is the place to head when you want to increase your Fire's features. Opened in March 2011, it was the biggest hint of all that Amazon was looking to build its own tablet computer. At the time it had slightly less than 4,000 applications in its catalogue, but this has since grown. It splits revenue with developers on a 70% / 30% basis, with the developers taking the larger proportion and Amazon retaining the rest to cover, among other things, merchant processing and advertising on its digital shelves. The store is currently

With its touch-sensitive 7in colour display, the Fire is a fully-fledged tablet computer, and more capable than its e-ink based Kindle siblings.

available in the US only, just like the Kindle Fire itself.

The App Store includes many of the titles that have proved big successes on rival platforms, such as Cut the Rope, Angry Birds and Autodesk's SketchBook Mobile. This, perhaps more than anything else (apart from its bargain price), makes the Fire the first serious competitor to Apple's market leading iPad 2.

Amazon Silk

Every Kindle includes a web browser. However, in the case of the regular Kindle, Kindle Touch and Kindle Keyboard, Amazon is very honest about it being an 'experimental' part of the ereader's operating system.

In the Kindle Fire the web browser is an integral and very important part of the way the device works. Although it doesn't include 3G connectivity, the Kindle Fire is designed as a take anywhere online device that lets you browse the web over wifi without unpacking your bulky notebook computer.

As we mentioned on the previous page, the Fire boasts a technology that Amazon has termed Silk, which uses the company's enormous cloud computing server farm to increase the speed at which you can browse the web.

As Amazon explains, a typical web page isn't merely a collection of text and images gathered from one single server. On average, each page you visit calls on around 80 files, which in turn are scattered across up to 13 different domains. These files include photos, text, stylesheets, remotely-hosted fonts and, of course, advertisements.

Many of these resources are actually hosted on Amazon's own servers, while others are hosted elsewhere, on servers with which Amazon's cloud computing intrastructure shares a direct series of fast connections.

Whenever you dial in the address of a page or click a link in the Fire's browser, therefore, it's sent to Amazon's Elastic Compute Cloud servers, which break down the request into smaller parts, working on which bits it would be faster for it to collect itself, and which bits your Fire should go off and find.

By splitting the workload in this way it shortens the time taken to reconstruct the page on your tablet's screen, making the whole thing feel more responsive and allowing you to get more done in less time.

Online content

Manufacturers have quickly come to the realisation that you don't buy a tablet for its specs; you buy it because of what it can do and, more

The Kindle Fire is a window on Amazon's world of digital content. Its store is perhaps the only one that can compete directly with Apple's offerings for its own tablet devices, the iPad and iPad 2, plus the iPhone and iPod touch.

importantly, what it can download. Like the iPad, the Kindle Fire is tied to its manufacturer's own online store, which gives Amazon a head start here. It has spent years building up a varied, yet integrated set of businesses, which together

form a virtual shopping mall through which you can buy movies, music and applications.

These are organised on the Kindle Fire's shelves and categorised using the tabs at the top of the screen.

Setting up your Kindle Fire

There are two ways to get content on to your Kindle Fire. By far the simplest method – and the one that Amazon would clearly prefer – is for you to buy it direct from its online store. To do this, you need to set up your wireless network.

All of the Kindle Fire's settings are organised through a centralised settings toolbar. Call this up by tapping the cog icon in the status bar at the top of the screen, followed by *Wi-Fi*. Tap *ON* to switch on the Fire's wireless features and it will automatically scan for available networks (*below left*).

Tap the name of your home or office network in the list, and the Fire will automatically detect the applicable security settings, asking you for the network password (*below centre*). Enter this and tap *Connect* to complete the process.

Every device on your network will be given a unique address, called an IP address, so that it can be accessed by other devices on the network and receive incoming data. If your network hasn't been set up with DHCP (Direct Host Control Protocol) to automatically provide every new device with an address, you'll need to enter your own details. Tap *Advanced Settings | Static IP settings*, followed by the *ON* button, and then enter your network settings.

At the bare minimum you'll need to provide the router address, subnet mask and an available IP address for your Kindle Fire (*below right*). You may need to ask your network administrator for these details, as the available IP address pool may be restricted for security purposes.

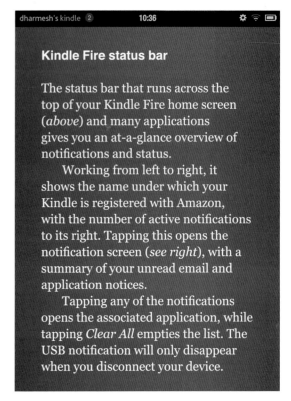

Kindle Fire status bar

The status bar that runs across the top of your Kindle Fire home screen (*above*) and many applications gives you an at-a-glance overview of notifications and status.

Working from left to right, it shows the name under which your Kindle is registered with Amazon, with the number of active notifications to its right. Tapping this opens the notification screen (*see right*), with a summary of your unread email and application notices.

Tapping any of the notifications opens the associated application, while tapping *Clear All* empties the list. The USB notification will only disappear when you disconnect your device.

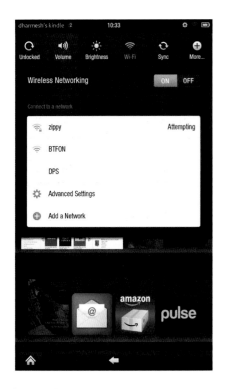

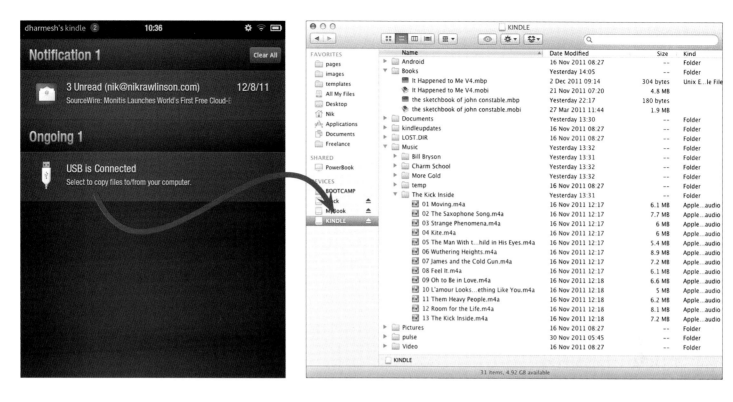

Manually adding media

The other way to get content onto your Kindle Fire is to manually drag it onto the device using Windows Explorer or the Mac Finder. Connect your Fire to your computer using USB, and if it doesn't automatically bring up the USB screen tap the notification icon, followed by *USB is Connected*. Your Fire will mount in your file system (*above*).

Just like a regular Kindle, the Fire's storage is split into sections for the various different media types. Drag your books, music, movies and photos into their respective folders and they will appear in the relevant applications on the Fire.

If your books don't appear in the books app then check in Documents, where they'll work in the same way as a regular Kindle download.

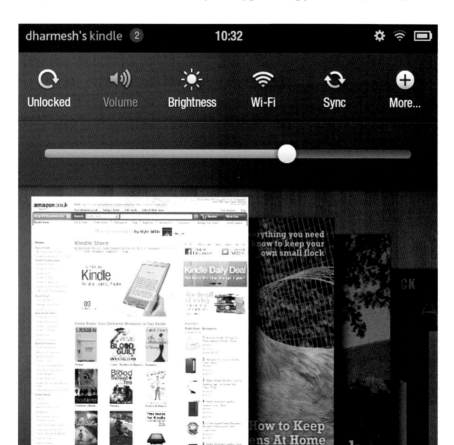

The multi-talented settings bar

The most commonly-used settings are organised on the settings bar, which first appears when you tap the cog icon. Cycle through them by tapping each one in turn and use the slider to change both the volume and brightness, depending on which you have selected.

The left-most icon, *Unlocked* in our grab (*left*) doesn't lock the Kindle itself, but stops the screen from reorientating itself as you move between portrait and landscape orientation. Tap it once to switch it on and again to release.

The full range of setting can be found by tapping the *More...* button to open the Settings application.

Set up an email account on your Kindle Fire

As well as a first class ebook reader and media playback device, the Kindle Fire is a fully-fledged tablet computer.

Running a heavily tweaked version of Google's Android operating system, it has an integrated email client with presets for the most common webmail account types. If you have your own self-hosted email account that isn't administered by one of those providers, you can also set it up using the 'Other' option. Check with your ISP which settings you need to enter in this case.

Although the Kindle Fire doesn't have a 3G option, so you can't use it when away from a wireless network, the email function makes the Kindle Fire a convenient means of accessing your email without firing up your desktop or laptop.

STEP BY STEP

1. When you first launch the email application, none of your accounts will be set up. Tap the button to start the process and then choose what kind of account you want to set up. If you have a regular POP3 or IMAP account from your ISP, select *Other*. If you're using one of the listed webmail accounts, tap its name.

2. Our email is hosted on Gmail, so we've tapped that entry and are now entering our email address and password. After tapping *Next* we select the server type. The options on offer are POP and IMAP. In this instance we want the latter so that our outgoing messages are

stored on the server and any messages we mark as read on the Fire are also marked as read on the server.

3. Settings will vary from provider to provider, but if you're setting up a Gmail account you can copy the details in grab three to set up your incoming server, remembering of course to enter your own username and password.

4. Likewise, you can copy these settings for the outgoing server if you're setting up a Gmail account, once again substituting our email address and password for your own.

5. Select how often you want your Kindle Fire to poll the server to collect new messages. By default it will only look when you manually tell it to do so, but you can change this to every 15, 30 or 60 minutes if you'd rather.

6. Finally, you need to enter your name using the format you'd like to have branding your messages, and give your account an identifiable name. In this case we've called ours Gmail so that we know which one it is.

7. And here's our email account up and running. Tap on a message to open it, and use the Newest drop-down at the top of the screen to change the order in which the messages are listed in your inbox.

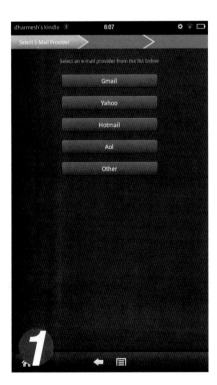

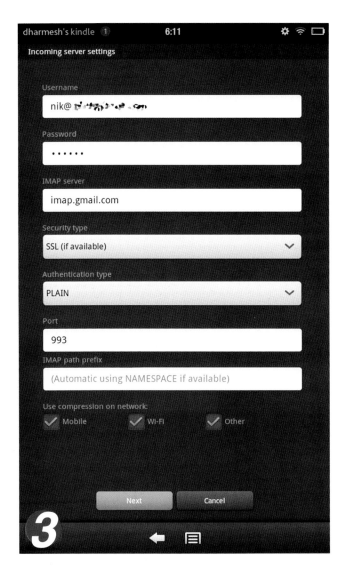

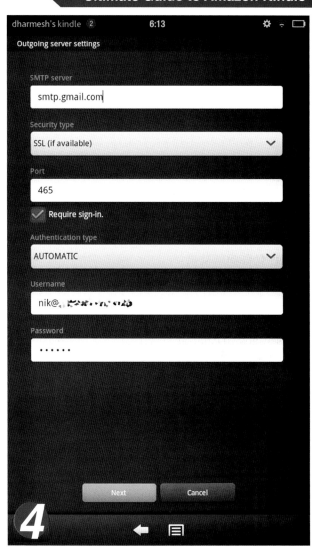

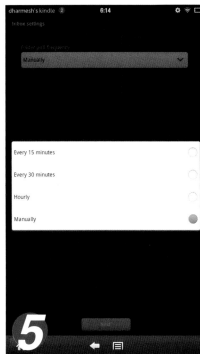

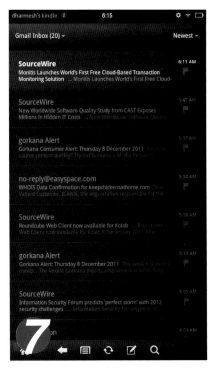

Purchasing and organising Kindle Fire applications

The Kindle Fire and Apple iPad are the leading tablet computers for one very good reason: they are both well supported by third-party developers who sell their wares through shops that are tied directly to each tablet's operating system.

The range of applications is impressive, and on the facing page we'll show you how to go about buying new apps for your Fire. Once you've got them on your device, though, it's important to understand how they are organised.

The Fire home screen is dominated by a large carousel shelf that organises each of your most recently-used applications, listened to albums, viewed films and read books. They are sorted in reverse order, with the most recent on the left and the others stacked below it. You can cycle through them by swiping left and right on whichever media appears at the top of the pile.

Although you may quit an application, it is usually still running in the background. If this is causing you problems – perhaps consuming too many system resources – then you can force it to quit fully by tapping *Settings* (the cog by the battery symbol) | *More* | *Applications*. Tap on the problem application, followed by *Force Stop*.

Below this carousel you'll see a number of shelves. These are where

Your most recently-used media and applications are stored on the large, upper shelf of your Kindle Fire home screen. Hold your finger on any you use frequently to call up the Add to Favourites tab (right) to add it to the lower bar, where it was stay until removed manually (far right).

you store your favourite applications and media so that you can access them quickly in the future. To add an item to one of the shelves, hold your finger on its icon in the carousel, or on the shelves in the Apps menu (found by tapping *Apps* on the home screen toolbar) and tap the *Add to Favourites* bubble tab that appears.

You can remove an application from your favourites by holding on its icon on the shelf and selecting *Remove from Favourites*.

Any apps that shipped as part of your Kindle Fire operating system are permanent residents and can't be deleted, but those you have downloaded can be deleted by selecting *Remove from Device* from this same menu. Holding your finger on a media item will instead give you a plain *Delete* option.

Applications are organised in the Apps tab, which you'll find on the toolbar on the front screen. You can organise them by how recently you have used them, or by name.

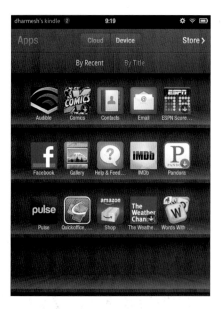

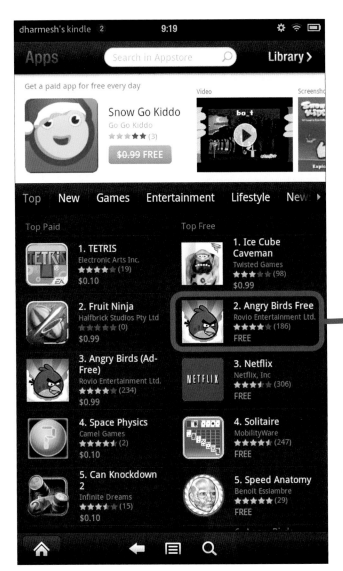

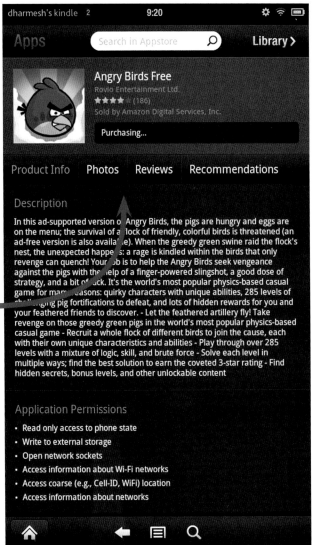

Buying applications

While the Kindle, Kindle Touch and Kindle Keyboard are sealed units that will only ever run the applications factory installed on them, the Kindle Fire is a fully-fledged tablet computer, backed up by a well-stocked Appstore.

Although you can view the store in a regular browser, if you want to install applications on your Kindle Fire you should access it directly from the home screen by tapping *Apps | Store*.

Applications are organised by category in tabs across the middle of the screen, just above the best-seller lists, and below the daily free application.

Use the search box at the top of the screen to search for particular keywords or application names and, when you find an app you're interested in, tap its name in the listing (*above left*), to open its full details (*above right*).

Each detailed entry includes a full description of the app, plus screen grabs (tap *Photos*), reviews and recommendations of other applications that you might like based on this purchase.

To download an application, tap its price at the top of the screen (or tap *FREE* if it doesn't have a price). This will change to *Buy App* or *Get App*, depending on whether or not it's charged for.

Tap this new button and the application will be automatically downloaded and installed on your Apps shelves, ready for use.

Note that even if you're downloading a free application you need to have up to date payment details registered with Amazon, so if your credit card has expired or your account doesn't have details tied to it you'll see an error box containing a link that you'll need to tap twice to visit your account and fix the problem.

The Kindle Fire itself also needs to be registered to your account. If it isn't, follow the instructions on page 22.

Downloading, organising and playing music

Amazon has long been a leading retailer of MP3 albums and singles. Naturally these are perfect for playing back using the Fire's built-in music application.

You won't find an icon for this as it's a core feature of the operating system. To access your tracks, therefore, tap Music on the home screen toolbar to open your library of playlists.

As well as playing your locally-stored tracks, the Fire can access tracks stored on the Amazon Cloud Drive. This is available only in the US at this time. All Cloud Drive accounts come with 5GB of free storage, but any tracks you buy from Amazon's MP3 store, which can be optionally sent to your Cloud Drive, won't count against this storage, effectively giving you unlimited free online music storage for anything bought through Amazon. Tracks bought through other stores and uploaded to the Cloud Drive will, however, be deducted from your available storage. If you exceed your 5GB limit with non-Amazon downloads, additional space can be bought at a price of $1 per gigabyte per year.

Switch between your local and remotely-stored tracks using the *Cloud* and *Device* buttons at the top of the playlist screen, then use the *Playlists*, *Artists*, *Albums* and *Songs* buttons to slice and dice your library in different ways to help you identify the track you're looking for. You can also search for tracks directly using the magnifier icon on the toolbar.

Amazon lets you audition every track before you buy it, courtesy of a 30-second sample.

Navigate the Music app

Album artwork This is bundled with the track or album when downloaded from Amazon, and transferred when copied over USB if transferring the tracks directly from your PC.

Shuffle Play the current album or playlist in a random order.

Volume slider Drag to change the volume. Note that this duplicates the volume slider in the settings bar, so any change you make here will affect the whole Fire system, not just the volume of played-back music.

Playlist button Tap to open the list of tracks on your currently-playing album and you can skip directly to the one you want to play next rather than stepping through them individually.

Progress bar Indicates your position within the track. Holding on the progress spot and dragging it left or right scrubs you back and forth through the track.

Repeat Continue playing the current playlist or album on a loop.

Toolbar The regular toolbar gives you access to your downloads, the option to retry a failed download, your settings and a shortcut to the 'Now Playing' screen.

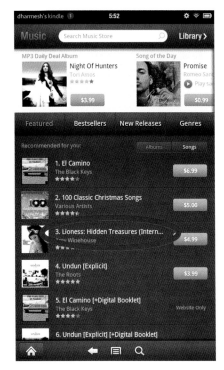
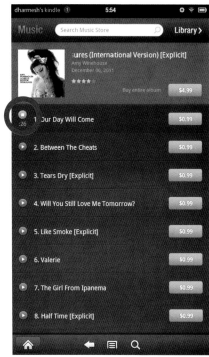

Buying music on your Kindle Fire: The Music app is tied directly to Amazon's MP3 store, allowing you to download music using 1-click purchase. Open the Store by tapping its link at the top of the Music player application (above, left), and tap an album name to open the full track listing. Every track is accompanied by a 30 second preview so you can audition it before making a purchase. Tap the play button to the left of a track to listen to it (above, centre). Buy individual tracks by tapping the price beside each one, or complete albums by tapping the price at the top of the screen beside the rating and description (above, right).

Building playlists

Playlists are sequences of tracks that you string together as though they were a virtual album. Each one can include singles and tracks from as many albums as you want, and can be shuffled and played on repeat in the same way as a regular album.

You can't drag playlists onto the Fire from a PC or Mac-based management application, but you can create them directly on the Fire itself.

Start by tapping the Playlists button on the Music toolbar and then press the *Create new playlist* line. Give your playlist a name so that it's easy to identify in the future (*below, left*) and tap Save to add it to your library.

You now need to choose which tracks should appear on that playlist. Remember there is no limit here, but as you can create a whole collection of playlists it makes sense to treat each one as though it were a Favourites lists in your contact book (see *p88*) and be selective, choosing tracks that go well together or suit a particular purpose for each playlist and leaving out poor fits.

To add a track, tap the '+' beside its name (*below, right*). Tap *Done* when you've finished and enjoy your playlist.

QUICK TIP

You can upload tracks to the Cloud Player using a regular browser. Point it at *amazon.com/clouddrive* and click on Music in the sidebar. If this is the first time you've used Cloud Drive you'll have to agree to the T&Cs, after which your 5GB of storage becomes available.

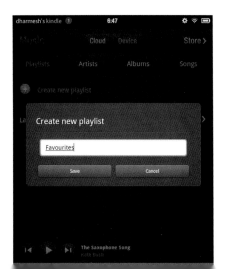
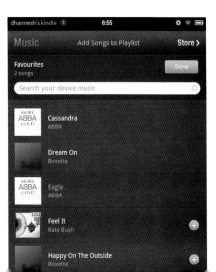

Videos on Kindle Fire

Every Kindle Fire comes with a free month's subscription to Amazon Prime. As well as offering free two-day delivery of all physical orders, regardless of size, and the option to borrow a book a month from the Kindle Owners' Lending Library, this also gives you access to unlimited streaming of over 10,000 commercial free movies and TV shows, including popular current series' like Glee, and modern classic movies, such as Notting Hill and You've Got Mail.

As one of the core media types available to Fire users through Amazon's online store, video has its own entry on the Kindle Home screen media menu. Tap it, followed by Store to visit the video shop.

This is split into TV and movies, with each divided into paid-for content – which numbers over 100,000 items – and free streamed Prime content.

You can't download Prime content to view offline unless you buy or rent it. It's purely a streamed offering, so you must have an active wifi connection to enjoy any movie or show in this collection. Simply tap *Watch Now*, sit back and relax (*see grab 1*).

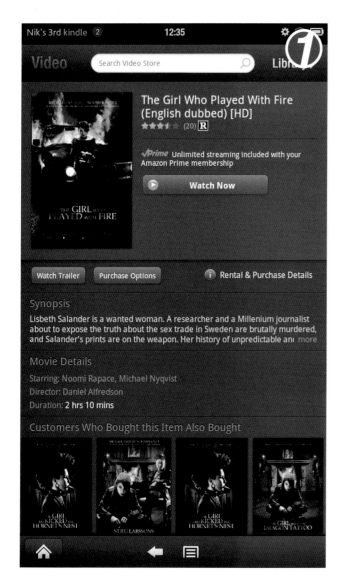

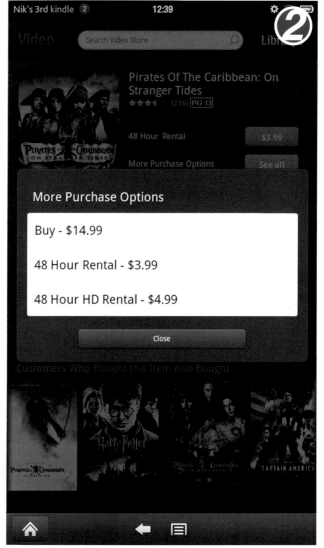

VIDEO PLAYER CONTROLS

Volume slider Drag left and right to adjust volume. Also affects system volume.

Skip back Rewind the video stream by exactly 10 seconds to repeat something you mayhave missed.

Transport control Quite simply, pause and resume playback.

Progress bar The full length of the bar indicates the length of the clip; the light grey portion is the part of the clip that has already been buffered from the server and the spot is your current position. Drag the spot to scrub back and forth within the clip.

Other content is available for renting or outright purchase, with full details hiding behind the *See all* button beside *More Purchase Options* (*grab 2*). Presently you can only take advantage of these purchase and rental options if you have a credit card issued in the US.

Note that although you can rent HD content, the Kindle Fire doesn't currently support HD video playback. The HD version will therefore be available for playback on other devices from your library, but the version you see on the Fire itself will be a regular standard-definition stream.

If you are renting content then the 48 hour (sometimes 24 hour) period stated on the rental options page denotes only the period during which you have to start watching the film or TV show. So long as you play some portion of it within that time you have 30 days in which to complete viewing the content.

You aren't restricted to viewing a video on the device through which you purchased it, so if you spot a great time-limited deal while you're browsing at work on your Kindle Fire, you can rent it right then to take advantage of the deal, but still view it on your computer – in HD should you choose – when you get back home. The Whispersync technology that synchronises your last-read page in a Kindle book also works with videos, retaining your viewing position in a video across multiple devices.

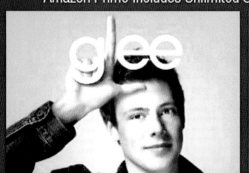

QUICK TIP

If you upload your own videos to the Fire they don't appear in the Video app. Instead, open Gallery (from your App shelves) and select the movie you want from there. Kindle Fire is compatible with H.263, H264 AVC and Mpeg 4 SP/ASP movie formats.

How to buy books with your Kindle Fire

The process of buying books through your Kindle Fire is broadly similar to that on a regular Kindle, except that the Books application doesn't have a native store of its own.

STEP BY STEP

1. Open the Books application. By default, the only book in your library will be a dictionary. Tap the *Store >* link to open Amazon's online catalogue.

2. This sends you to the Fire's built-in browser and opens the Amazon homepage, with the media type drop-down set to Kindle Store. Use the search box to type in the name of the book you want to read, the author you're searching for, or keywords that describe your chosen book. When your chosen book appears in the list of results, tap its title to open the full listing.

3. Tap on the *Delivery to:* drop-down menu and select the Kindle on which you want to read the book. This applies the necessary Digital Rights Management measures to your download.

4. Your Kindle will now be listed in the *Deliver to:* menu. Tap the *Buy now with 1-Click* button to buy the book without any further confirmation. It will now be downloaded to your device, and will be filed in the Books application, ready to be read.

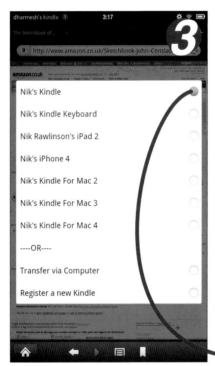

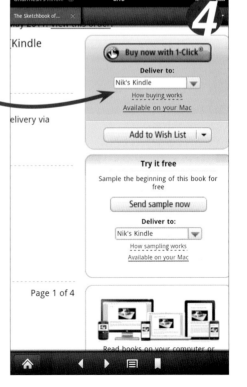

QUICK TIP

Books, just like applications, can be added to the shelves of your favourites that appear on the Fire home screen. Adding your current book to your Favourites helps you find it quickly whenever you sit down to read. Hold your finger on the cover of your book and select *Add to Favourites* to place it on your home screen shelves.

Kindle Fire Newsstand

Just as more of us than ever are now reading books online, so online and digital magazines are becoming increasingly popular.

Various papers and magazines are already available on the Kindle Keyboard, Kindle and Kindle Touch, and now Amazon is building on this solid foundation by opening a dedicated Kindle Fire Newsstand. At present, this is available only to Kindle Fire users in the US. In other countries in which traditional e-ink-based Kindles are on sale, a smaller range of non-interactive titles are available through local territorial stores.

The Newsstand features over 400 full colour magazines, including a host of well-known titles including Wired, Elle, Good Housekeeping, Popular Mechanics and Reader's Digest. As well as replicating most titles as you would expect to see them in print, many are presented as enhanced editions with interactive content and live media.

You can sample each of them in advance courtesy of a 14 day free trial.

Amazon has also built a magazine store for readers using a Kindle app on an alternative Android tablet computer. Although there's access to a narrower range of titles – 100 magazines and newspapers – each of these can be synchronised between devices (in the same way as books) so that whichever device you choose to read on, you'll benefit from continuing to read from the same page you left off, thanks to Amazon's Whispersync technology.

To make this possible, Amazon has offered publishers some very

attractive terms, including a 70% share of the cover price – more than they would earn when selling a traditional printed magazine in a shop in most cases – on the condition that they allow customers to read each publication on any device in all countries where the publisher has the rights to publish that magazine.

Magazines are bought on subscription rather than an issue-by-issue basis, with charges applying after the free trial.

QUICK TIP

If the magazine you want to read isn't available on the Kindle Newsstand, check out the Kindle Fire Zinio application from the Appstore. Zinio is an alternative digital publishing platform popular around the world, offering an almost unrivalled choice of magazines from a host of international publishers, including popular titles such as *PC Pro* and *MacUser*.

How to use Amazon Cloud Drive

Cloud Drive is Amazon's online file storage facility. It allows anyone with an Amazon account to store up to 5GB of files online, to be accessed from any web-connected computer – and the Kindle Fire.

If you have an Amazon account, you already have a Cloud Drive account; to sign in, point a regular desktop or laptop browser at *https://www.amazon.com/clouddrive* and use your regular Amazon login credentials.

Amazon allows access to the Cloud Drive from up to eight different devices. However, as it uses cookies to track some of these devices, such as browsers, be aware you may use up one of your allocation by clearing out your cookie cache, so if you use the service with a regular browser be careful to only clear out your cookies selectively, rather than wiping the whole directory.

Visiting your Cloud Drive from different browsers on the same computer will also use up more of your Cloud Drive device allocations.

Cloud Drive is Amazon's online storage service. Each account comes with a free allocation of 5GB of space for documents, pictures, music and video. Unchanged MP3s bought from Amazon don't eat into your storage space.

Changing your plan

Although 5GB is a generous amount of space for Amazon to give away for free – particularly considering how many people are eligible for the service – it's still frighteningly easy to fill it quickly in these days of multi-gigabyte video files, office documents and backups.

Amazon therefore makes it easy to buy additional storage, with six tiered plans available to anyone who wants to build on the bundled 5GB.

This option is not currently available in all territories (see our

Quick Tip, right), but in those where it is the additional storage will be available immediately.

Unless you cancel the plan or downgrade it at a later date, it will be automatically renewed to your new level at the start of your next billing cycle, so it's important to keep an eye on your anniversary dates to avoid unexpected bills.

Should you later decide to downgrade your plan the additional storage will remain available until your billing cycle renewal, when it will be removed without charge.

Below: Signing up is free, so long as you agree to the T&Cs.

SHOPPING LIST

Cloud Drive storage plan prices:

5GB.	..	..	Free
20GB	..	..	$20 per year
50GB	..	..	$50 per year
100GB	..	..	$100 per year
200GB	..	..	$200 per year
500GB	..	..	$500 per year
1000GB..		..	$1000 per year

Deleting files

When you delete a file, it remains in place but is moved to the trash. It therefore continues to occupy space on your Cloud Drive. You can see how much space it is using by navigating your browser to: *https://www.amazon.com/clouddrive/manage/*.

To clear out these items and thus increase your available storage space without buying extra capacity, return to your Cloud Drive home page, click *Deleted Items* in the left-hand margin and then click *Permanently Delete All*.

Amazon Cloud Player

Cloud Drive users in the United States can also use Amazon Cloud Player to stream their MP3 purchases and any tracks they have uploaded to their Cloud Drive without first downloading them. It works from any computer or Android device with Internet access. Visit *www.cloudplayer.com* to log in and access your music.

If you try to access this site from outside of the US, you will currently see a warning that Cloud Player is not available in your territory. Likewise, should you tap the Cloud tab in the Music app it won't see your uploaded music, and instead present you with a button directing you to *Shop in the Music store*.

Not only a repository for your documents and music, the Cloud tabs on many of the Kindle Fire applications let you access your previously-purchased content from Amazon's servers. Here, the Books Cloud tab shows volumes we have bought on our other Kindle devices, allowing us to download them again on our Kindle Fire without purchasing a second copy. Books don't appear in the Cloud Drive web view.

QUICK TIP

Upgrades to the 5GB free storage space are currently unavailable in the following countries:

Austria	Belgium	Bulgaria	Cyprus
Czech Republic	Denmark	Estonia	Finland
France	Germany	Greece	Hungary
Ireland	Italy	Latvia	Lithuania
Luxembourg	Malta	Netherlands	Poland
Portugal	Romania	Slovakia	Slovenia
Spain	Sweden	United Kingdom	

Source: Amazon.com

Documents

When you email a document to your Kindle it is now automatically saved to your Kindle Library. Although this uses up space that you might prefer not to lose when all you want to do is post a document to one particular Kindle, it does make it available to all of your other devices. Note that your Kindle Library is different to the Cloud Drive, being the catalogue of books you have previously downloaded.

QUICK TIP

If your music doesn't appear on the Music app's Cloud tab within ten minutes, force it to check for available downloads by tapping Refresh Cloud Drive (*below*).

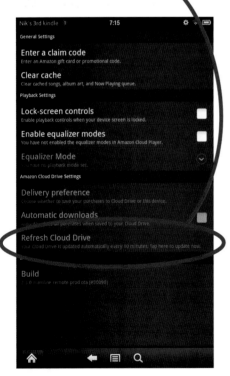

How to buy music and upload it to your Cloud Drive

Skill level	Beginner – a simple task that everyone can complete
Time required	Around ten minutes
Equipment required	Compatible browser (Internet Explorer 7 or later; latest versions of Firefox, Chrome or Safari); JavaScript, Flash and an active Amazon account with up to date billing data in place.

STEP BY STEP

1. Download a copy of the Amazon MP3 Downloader from *http://www.amazon.com/gp/dmusic/help/amd.html*. Once installed, this will pop up every time you buy MP3s from Amazon, filing them neatly on your hard drive and, if set up correctly, adding them to third-party music players, such as iTunes.

    Now head online to Amazon's MP3 store and search for the tracks or album you want to download. When you find what you're after, buy it using the 1-Click method (which will apply any available gift certificate balance currently available on your account) or use the regular step-by-step process and complete the transaction. The Downloader will now pop up and manage the downloading and filing of your tracks.

2. Customers in the US will see their music appear in the Cloud Drive within 10 minutes of making a purchase. Log in to the Drive and click *Your Amazon MP3 Purchases* in the upper left box to find them. Shoppers from outside of the US must manually upload the tracks themselves.

    To do this, log in at *https://www.amazon.com/clouddrive/* and click *Music*, followed by *Upload Files*. If you haven't uploaded anything to the Cloud Drive before you'll have to agree to Amazon's Terms and Conditions before you can proceed any further.

3. With the Terms and Conditions accepted, click *Select files to upload...* and navigate to your downloads on your hard drive. Select the files you want to upload and click Open.

4. You'll be returned to the Cloud Drive upload dialogue where the selected files are listed in order. As the uploader sends each one to the server you'll see how quickly it's progressing courtesy of a bar that fills up. The speed at which it does this will depend on the speed of your broadband connection, but in our experience, on a domestic connection, a 15-track album completed the transfer from local drive to Cloud Drive in a little over five minutes. Once in place, you'll find the files by clicking Music in the Cloud Drive's left-hand boxes.

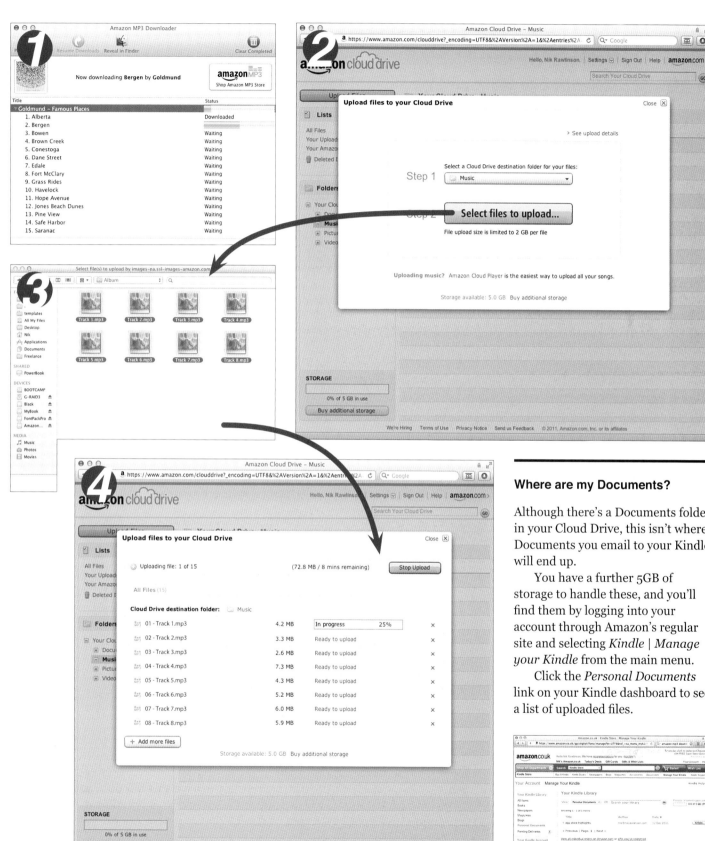

Where are my Documents?

Although there's a Documents folder in your Cloud Drive, this isn't where Documents you email to your Kindle will end up.

You have a further 5GB of storage to handle these, and you'll find them by logging into your account through Amazon's regular site and selecting *Kindle | Manage your Kindle* from the main menu.

Click the *Personal Documents* link on your Kindle dashboard to see a list of uploaded files.

Working on the move

Even without investing in any third-party applications, you can use your Kindle Fire to work on the move. With a built-in email client it's the perfect tool for keeping in touch with colleagues when all you need to do is quickly check your inbox, and thanks to the pre-installed edition of Quickoffice, which we'll explore in greater depth shortly, you can read previously saved documents, either on your Kindle's storage or online, whenever you have a spare moment.

Over the page we'll walk you through the process of setting up your Kindle address book and importing contact details from your PC or Mac using the industry standard vCard format, which will let you keep your addresses in sync, whichever device you choose to use as your primary source.

Using Quickoffice

The Kindle Fire includes a pre-installed copy of Quickoffice. This is a cut-down version of the highly regarded Quickoffice Pro, which is available as an upgrade from the Amazon Appstore for $9.99 (follow the update link from within the application itself).

Although this doesn't let you create original documents or edit those that have been installed on the Fire by dragging them over USB, it does let you view documents you have created elsewhere, and even those you have stored online. This means that whenever you have a wifi connection you can use your Kindle Fire to gem up on notes, refer to spreadsheets or run colleagues through a presentation without reverting to your laptop.

Here we're going to walk through the process of accessing documents stored in our Google Docs account. The process will differ slightly for each of the supported online services, but by following these principles you should have no trouble accessing your data.

1. Tap the Quickoffice Accounts button and choose the service for the account to which you want to link. Dropbox, box, Huddle and SugarSync are synchronisation tools through which you can access documents you have copied to the server. Google Docs is an online office suite, meaning you can work directly with your files through the browser (including the Fire's own browser) and view them using Quickoffice.

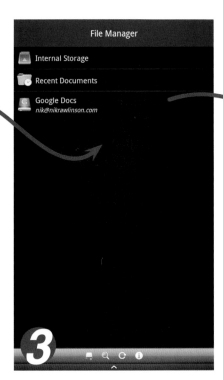

QUICK TIPS

Select several documents at once by ticking the checkboxes to the right of each one, and then use the toolbar at the bottom of the screen to perform multiple operations simultaneously. This allows you to, for example, email documents from one of your online accounts using the Fire's integrated email application without first downloading them and attaching them to a message (*left*). In the same way, you can copy, cut and paste whole documents using the clipboard by selecting their checkboxes and then tapping the appropriate icons on the toolbar. This lets you perform server-side tasks without logging in through the Fire's Silk browser.

MobileMe is an online service operated by Apple, which the company is currently in the process of phasing out as it transitions to iCloud.

2. Each service requires that you log in with a valid set of credentials. If you don't already have an account for any of them, visit their respective websites and sign up for a free. Otherwise, enter your username (often your email address) and the password you chose during the registration process, and then tap OK.

3. Quickoffice will use your credentials to log in to your account and, assuming all went well, add your account to the File Manager as though it was another form of internal storage.

4. Tap your account in the File Manager to open up the full directory listing, showing all of your documents and the folders into which they are organised. Files compatible with one of the three Quickoffice applications are given a matching icon.

5. Tap the document you want to open in the Quickoffice file viewer. Although you can scroll through them and switch between pages on spreadsheets, this is a viewer in the purest sense of the word, so you can't edit anything.

Managing your contacts

The Kindle Fire includes a built-in contacts manager, which ties in with the email application to feed in your contact details when you start typing their names in the To, CC or BCC fields of a new message.

The easiest way to do this is usually to start typing the first few letters of a contact's name, at which point the result will continue to refine itself until you find the person you need. Alternatively, tap the yellow '+' at the end of the field to open your contact book and select the name you need.

Adding a new contact is a simple matter of typing the relevant details into the address card boxes in the contacts application (*right*). Once saved they are available to other applications on your Kindle, and can be exported in the industry-standard vCard format. By reversing the process, you can import your contacts from your Mac or PC.

STEP BY STEP

1. Use your desktop's contacts application to select the contacts you want to copy to your Fire and export them using vCard format. Save them to your desktop and then connect your Kindle Fire. Ensure it is mounted in the Mac Finder or Windows Explorer, then open any of its folders and copy your exported contacts file across. We have chosen to put ours in the Documents folder, just to keep things tidy.

2. Turning to your Kindle, open the Contacts application and tap the menu button at the foot of the screen, followed by *Import / Export*. Select *Import from internal storage* and your Fire will search its file system for your saved file without you having to tell it where it is.

3. If you have several individual vCard files on your Kindle you can import them all at once, but we don't want to do that – we only want to import the most recent update to our address book. In this case we'll leave it set to the default – *Import one vCard file* – and tap OK to proceed.

4. Our Fire has found two vCard files in its file system. One of these – the one preceded by the dot – is a hidden system file, which we can safely ignore. We have therefore selected the second file and tapped OK to import its contents.

5. Because vCard files follow a common format, with each piece of data accurately described, the Fire Contacts application and any other app that can import the format can separate out names, addresses, phone numbers, email details and so on, and use them to populate its database.

Contacts shows a progress meter as it imports your contacts and, when it's finished, returns you to your contacts list with each entry now filed in alphabetical order.

Adding contacts to your address book is a simple matter of tapping their details into the labelled boxes.

Setting favourites

There are some contacts that you will use more than others, and so it pays to make them easier to find. You can therefore set them as favourites in the same way that you'd set favourite applications.

Open a contact's complete record by tapping the name in the

Once you have added a contact to your address book, typing their name into the email application swaps it out for their full address.

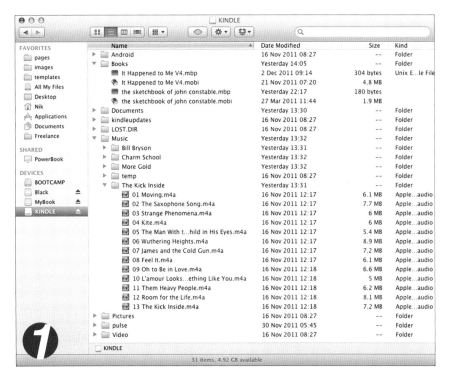

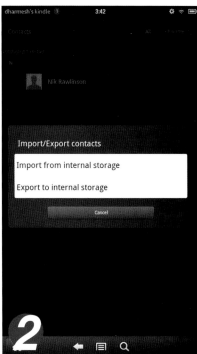

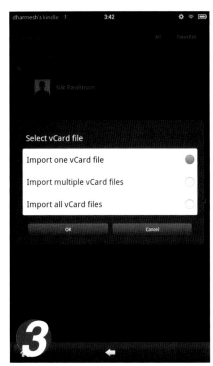

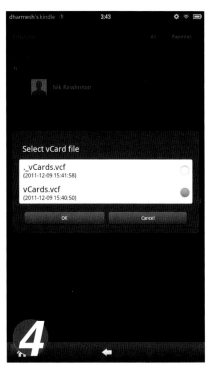

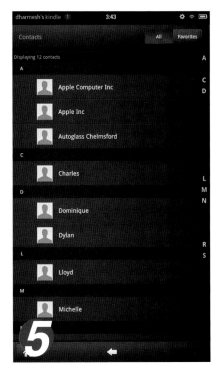

address book listing and then tap the star at the top of the screen to mark it as a favourite.

You can set as many contacts as you want as favourites, although for obvious reasons it pays to set only a handful, as setting a large number of favourites will be ineffective in

trying to strip down your contacts list to a more manageable number of entries.

In future, when you want to find your most often used contacts, open the application and tap the *Favourites* button to view only your marked contacts.

QUICK TIP

Rather than scrolling through your contacts, use the magnifying glass on the toolbar to open the search box, or tap on the individual letters in the right hand margin to skip directly to that initial.

Kindle Fixer

Kindle troubleshooter

■ **Registration and hardware issues**

I bought my Kindle second hand and it's still registered to the previous user. Help!

You need to deregister the Kindle and tie it to your account instead (although the person who sold it should have done this for you, for their own security).

On an e-ink based Kindle press the menu button and then select *Settings | deregister*. Kindle Fire users, tap *Settings | More | My Account | Deregister*.

If you bought someone a Kindle as a present it will be registered to your account unless you marked it as a gift. You'll need to deregister it yourself before they can start using it. Do this by logging into your Amazon account through the browser and selecting *Kindle | Manage Your Kindle* in the left-hand margin. The next page will display a *Deregister* link beside the gifted Kindle.

You'll now find the Register option in the same position, or follow the instructions on p22 to register the Kindle through your Amazon account in a browser.

I've forgotten my e-ink Kindle's password.

If you've set a password to stop unauthorised users viewing your downloads, it's very important that you don't forget it, as the only way to get back in to your device is to reset the whole thing. As a final resort, switch on your Kindle in the usual way and enter *resetmykindle* in the

password box. This will get you back in, but only after deleting all of your content. However, as this will all be backed up on Amazon's servers you'll be able to download it again from there.

How do I switch off my Kindle?

So long as you've switched off their wifi and 3G features, regular e-ink (i.e. non-Fire) Kindles don't use any more power when in standby than they do when you're reading a page; power is consumed when you turn pages and it has to change the e-ink composition.

However, if you are planning on taking a long journey and want to switch it off entirely while you're away then holding the

power switch for 20 seconds will shut it down entirely, blanking the screen so that not even the screensavers show.

My Kindle won't switch on

Most likely this is happening because your battery needs recharging. If your Kindle shipped with a plug, plug it in and leave it to charge overnight. If you don't have a plug, connect it to the USB port of a switched-on computer and again leave it for several hours to top up the battery.

Unplug the Kindle and hold the power switch for several seconds. If it still doesn't work, contact Amazon. Your Kindle is covered by a 12-month limited warranty.

Although Amazon gives each of your Kindles a name when you register it, you can choose an alternative to make buying and downloading books less confusing if you have more than one device.

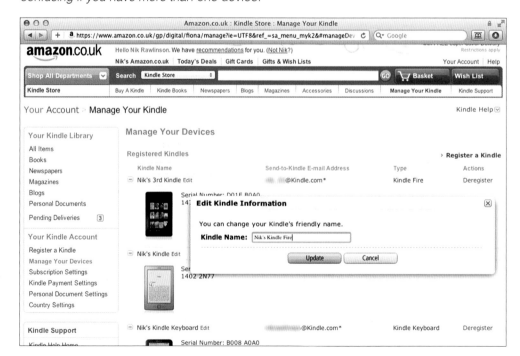

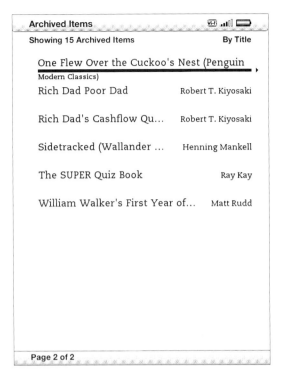

■ Transferring and syncing content

How do I copy my existing Kindle content to my new Kindle?

There's no need to copy everything over when you buy a new Kindle, as Amazon stores all of your purchases in your library.

To enjoy the same books on your new Kindle as you did on your old one, make sure your wifi connection is active and select *Menu | View Archived Items* to call up a list of your books (*above left*). You can then retrieve any of the ones you want on your new device and they'll appear on the Home screen.

On the Kindle Fire, simply open the Books application and tap the Cloud button to view your past purchases. Each one will be

How do I change the name of my Kindle?

Every Kindle registered to your account has its own unique name, which appears in the menu of destination options from which you can choose when sending books to your device.

Amazon picks this name for you when you first register your Kindle, but if you'd rather use something else, you can change it. Log in to your Amazon account using a regular browser and click *Kindle | Manage My Kindle | Manage Your Devices*. Now click Edit beside the name of the Kindle you want to rename and type in the new details (see grab, *left*).

How do I get rid of the adverts from my Kindle sleep screen?

If you bought a Kindle with 'Special Offers' you paid a subsidised price, as you would for a mobile phone on an ongoing contract. You can't remove the adverts, so your only option would be to buy a new Kindle without offers.

How do I update my Kindle software?

From time to time Amazon updates the operating system for its Kindles – both current models and legacy devices. These updates patch security issues, improve performance and sometimes add new features. You can find the latest updates for your Kindle, including details of how you go about installing them, at *http://amzn.to/suutAb*.

My Kindle operating system has somehow been set to a foreign language I don't understand. How do I change it back?

The most recent batch of Kindles support German, Spanish, French, Italian, Portugese and two versions of English (British and American). If you have accidentally changed your language setting on an e-ink Kindle and so don't understand the menus to change it back, press Menu, navigate to the second screen and then choose the first menu option to pick an alternative (*see right*).

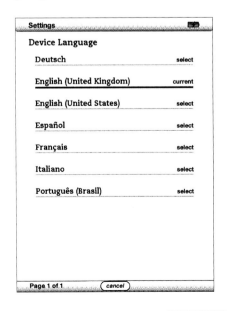

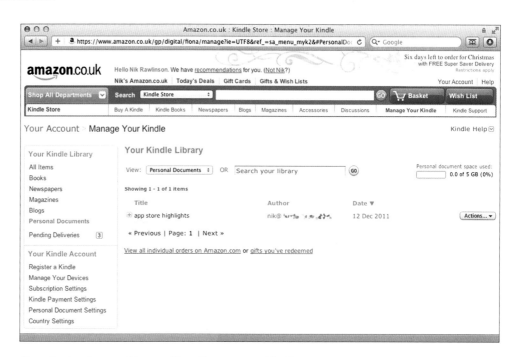

accompanied by a down-pointing arrow. Tap it to load the book onto your new Kindle.

How to I change my Kindle email address?

This is the address to which you email documents that you want to transfer to your Kindle without dragging them across over USB. Amazon sets one for you when you first register your Kindle, with the extension @*kindle.com*.

If you want to choose a more memorable address, log in to your Amazon account using a regular browser and click *Kindle | Manage My Kindle | Personal Document Settings*.

From this screen, click Edit beside the address of the Kindle for which you want to change the address and enter a new username in front of the @ symbol. You can't change the *kindle.com* part of the address.

While here you should also check the list of authorised addresses allowed to send content to your Kindles to ensure that you have removed any old, out of date entries, and included any address from which you would conceivably send content to your device.

I've emailed a file to my Kindle but it's still not appeared. Where is it?

First, check that your Kindle has an active network connection and that the address from which you sent the file is authorised to access the device (*see above*). If neither of these is at issue, force it to check for

If you're having trouble emailing files to your Kindle, log in to your account and check your Personal Documents folder. If your file doesn't appear there, ask your ISP whether it's experiencing any mail connection problems.

new content by pressing the Menu button and selecting *Sync & Check for Items*.

If this doesn't bring down your file, then you need to make sure that you sent a file type supported by your Kindle. See the box entitled *Supported File Types*, on the facing page, here.

Finally, check the size of your file. Amazon has wisely placed restrictions on the maximum file size that can be transferred to your device in this way. No file can consume more than 50MB of disk space, and you mustn't attach more than 25 documents to a single email, nor address that email to more than 15 different @*kindle.com* or @*free. kindle.com* addresses.

Finally, log in to your Amazon account using a regular browser and navigate to *Kindle | Manage Your Kindle | Personal Documents* to see whether your file has even been received at your Kindle address. If not, the problem is likely to be at your local end of the transfer. Check for mail problems with your Internet Service Provider (ISP).

I'm reading the same book on two devices, or a Kindle and a Kindle app, and the pages are out of sync on each device. Why?

Check that both of your devices have an active network connection and can connect to the Internet. They need this to send their current page position, along with any annotations and bookmarks, back to Amazon using Whispersync. In the other direction, they also use it to download any page positions set when reading on companion devices.

If two people are reading the same book bought through the same Amazon account but on different devices, be sure to switch off wifi to avoid each reader interfering with their partner's position in their own copy of the book.

Bear in mind, also, that keeping your wifi or 3G connection active will drain your battery at a quicker rate, so if you are reading your book on one device it makes sense to keep it switched off unless you specifically need web access.

When you connect your Kindle to your PC or Mac it mounts as an external storage device.

You should therefore follow accepted good practice and make sure you safely eject from the Task Bar tray on Windows, or from the Finder sidebar on the Mac (as illustrated by the red circle, left), before disconnecting it from your computer. This avoids any data corruption.

SUPPORTED FILE TYPES

The Kindle supports the following file types when transferring documents and files by email:

- Word .doc and .docx
- HTML
- Rich Text Format
- JPEG
- Gif
- PNG
- Bitmap (.bmp)
- PDF
- Kindle format (.azw)
- Mobipocket (.mobi)

When transferring files over USB it enjoys greater file type support, adding the following to those detailed above:

- AAC audio
- AAC+ audio
- Enhanced AAC+ audio
- .3gp audio
- Ogg Vorbis
- Midi
- MP3
- Wave format (.wav)
- H.263 video
- H264 AVC video
- MPEG4
- VP8 video

■ Music

I've bought some MP3s from Amazon and they aren't showing up on my Kindle Fire.

Tracks you have recently purchased can take up to 10 minutes to show up on the Cloud tab of the Music app, as they're being synced on the server in the background. You can hurry along the process in a similar way to forcing a Kindle to check for incoming documents by tapping *Music | Menu* (the line-filled rectangle at the bottom of the screen) | *Settings | Refresh Cloud Drive* (see below).

Note that music streaming isn't available outside of the US, so MP3 downloads won't appear on the Cloud tab for non-US users.

When I connect my Kindle to my computer, I can't see a Music folder in its memory.

Not all Kindles have a music folder by default, but that's not a problem as you can create one yourself using your Mac or PC and from there drag content into it.

Note, however, that not all Kindles have music and audio playback features. The entry level Kindle, for example, can't play audio as it doesn't have speakers or a headphone socket – even if you bought the non-subsidised version without the special offers. It therefore doesn't support any audio file types and so creating and populating a music folder would be a waste of your limited storage.

■ End of life

I've finished with my Kindle.

There's plenty to do with an old Kindle. Sell it, keep it as a spare, give it away to friends, donate it to a charity shop. If for any reason none of those options suits you, be earth friendly and recycle it.

US-based Kindle owners can navigate via their browser to: *ecotakeback.com/kindle* to find Amazon's official recycling partner, print out a label and send it off to be turned into something else. Don't forget to deregister it first.

Delivery preference
Choose whether to save your purchases to Cloud Drive or this device.

Automatic downloads
Auto-download all purchases when saved to your Cloud Drive.

Refresh Cloud Drive
Your Cloud Drive is updated automatically every 10 minutes. Tap here to update now.

Info

Build
2.3.0 mainline remote prod ota (#30098)

Glossary

The Kindle may have been designed with ease of use in mind, but it still lives in a world of acronyms and jargon. To really get along with your e-reader, there are a few words and phrases you ought to know, starting with these.

3G Third-generation mobile phone network technology offering speeds high enough to enable rudimentary video conferencing and mobile television streaming. It is widely available across much of Europe, but was first introduced for public consumption in Japan in 2001. It is used on some regular Kindle devices for buying content and performing web tasks.

802.11a/b/g/n Wireless communications standards. See *wifi*.

Amazon Silk Browser on the Kindle Fire that splits the work involved in requesting and assembling the various parts of a web page between the tablet device and Amazon's cloud computing network. As much of the content of the pages you view will already be cached on the cloud network, having been requested by other users, you should experience a significantly faster browsing experience overall.

Appstore Online shop distributing free and charged-for applications for use on a portable device such as the Kindle Fire, giving users an easy to find, trusted outlet.

Bitrate Means of expressing the number of audio samples processed in a set period of time, usually a second. See also *kilobits per second*.

Cloud A term for the centralised computing network that is most often used as a virtual storage device. Amazon's cloud infrastructure performs two functions: it's a place to store your book, music and video purchases (so that they don't always need to be kept on your device), and it's a place where some of the Kindle Fire's processing functions are carried out to take the strain off your tablet.

Compression When images on a website or music on a Kindle are made smaller so that they either download more quickly or take up less space in the device's memory they are said to have been compressed. Compression involves selectively removing parts of the file that are less easily seen or heard by the human eye and ear, and simplifying the more complex parts.

Digital Rights Management (DRM). Additional encoded data added to a digitised piece of audio or video, or a book, that controls the way in which it will work, usually preventing it from being shared among several users.

e-ink Screen technology used in all Kindles except for the Kindle Fire. Uses reflected light rather than being backlit and so is often easier to read in bright light than an LCD equivalent. Currently monochrome, but colour editions are being developed.

Encoding The process of capturing an analogue data source, such as a sound or an image, and translating it into a digital format. Although files can be encoded with no loss of quality, the process usually also involves compression to reduce file sizes.

Firewall Hardware or software device that controls the flow of data in and out of a machine or network. It can also help to rebuff attacks from hackers. Frequently used by network administrators to ensure that local users do not access external services that could compromise the integrity of the network.

Firmware Software built into a device such as the Kindle that controls all of its core functions. The closest equivalent in a regular computer is the operating system that hosts the various applications it runs. Windows, Linux and Mac OS X are three examples. Amazon has released the source code for the Kindle's operating system so that it can be downloaded and examined by the general public, and also delivers periodic updates that add new features to its devices.

GB Gigabyte. One billion bytes, and a means of measuring the capacity of a device. A byte is made up of eight bits, and a bit is equivalent to a single character, such as a, b, c, 4, 5, 6 and so on. As digital files are encoded using the characters 0 and 1, each digit that makes up part of its encoding will represent one bit, every eight characters will make one byte, every 1,024 bytes will equal a kilobyte and every million kilobytes will equate to a gigabyte (allowing for rounding).

Home Screen As used within this guide, the term used to describe the screen within the various Kindle interfaces that displays the icons for the various installed applications (on Kindle Fire) or the books and other media content that you have downloaded (e-ink-based Kindles).

HTML Acronym for HyperText Mark-up Language, the code used to program web pages. It is a plain-English language code, which uses simple tags such as <b> to denote bold, <i> to instigate italics and <p> to mark the start of a paragraph. Several applications, such as Adobe Dreamweaver, greatly simplify the task of writing web pages by allowing programmers to work in a desktop publishing-style layout mode, rather than having to manipulate raw code. HTML is often supplemented by attached styling information in the form of Cascading Style Sheets (CSS). Browsers combine the two to construct a page.

IMAP Internet Message Access Protocol. A server-based means of hosting incoming and outgoing email messages such that they can be accessed using a remote client such as the email application on the Kindle Fire. The primary benefit of working in this way is that the messages will always be accessible from any device, anywhere and at any time.

Kilobits per second (Kbps) A measurement of the number of audio samples that go to make each second of music in a digitally encoded track. The higher this number, the smoother

the sound wave will be, and the truer to the original it will sound.

MP3 Shorthand term used to denote audio tracks encoded using the Motion Picture Expert Group codec 2 (Mpeg-2), level three. Arguably the most common audio format found on the web thanks to its widespread use by portable music players. Capable of being read by most Kindle devices.

OS X Operating system developed by Apple, a variant of which is used inside the iPhone and later versions of the iPod under the name iOS. Like Microsoft Windows, It allows Kindle users to interact with their e-reader using USB, and is mounted as though a hard drive onto, which they can drag downloaded content.

Playlist Menu of audio tracks or video files waiting to be played.

Podcast Pre-recorded audio or video programme distributed over the Internet and optimised for playback on portable devices such as the Kindle Fire. Initially considered to be solely of interest to bedroom broadcasters, podcasts have since been embraced by newspaper titles such as The Guardian and The Times in the UK, as well as international broadcasters

like the BBC, which makes much of its spoken content – from both Radio 4 and its popular networks – available in the format. Video podcasts are sometimes called vodcasts.

Pop3 Post Office Protocol 3. This is the predominant technology for email delivery used by most consumer-level Internet service providers. All good email clients, including the one built into the Kindle Fire, can use this protocol to receive email.

Push email The technology by which emails are sent from the central server that holds them to a client device, such as a mobile phone or BlackBerry, without the owner having to manually instigate a retrieval for their messages.

Rip A term used to described the act of extracting audio from a CD for digital playback from a computer, or portable device. 'She ripped the CD to play on her Kindle Fire'.

RSS Rich Site Summary, or Really Simple Syndication, depending on who you're talking to. RSS is a means of presenting the content of a web page without the layout and design so it can be integrated into other sites or read in dedicated applications called aggregators. Google Reader (*reader.*

google.com) is an example of a web-based application. RSS aggregation remains a common, but infrequently used feature on many mobile phones.

SMTP Simple Mail Transfer Protocol. This is the most common – almost default – means of sending email from any client that works on the basis of composing messages using a standalone client rather than a web-based system.

SSL Secure Sockets Layer. A method used to encrypt data sent across wireless connections and the Internet so that it is less easy for uninvited third parties to intercept and decode .

Sync Short for *sync*hronise. The means of swapping data and purchases between the Kindle and Amazon's network. Traditionally performed using Amazon's Whispersync technology, although you can also transfer content manually by connecting your Kindle to your computer and dragging it across.

USB Universal Serial Bus. A socket, plug and cable system that allows almost any peripheral to be connected to a Mac or PC, including printers, mice, keyboards and so on. The Kindle also uses USB as a means of exchanging media content with a computer when connected physically and, now that Amazon is not shipping plugs with most of its Kindle products, also a connection through which you can charge your device.

VBR Variable Bit Rate. A means of varying the effective audio resolution of a sound file, such as a song, based on the complexity of its contents.

WAV Short for *WAV*eform audio format. A format used to store audio developed initially by Microsoft and IBM. It remains more popular on Windows computers than Macs and can be played back by some Kindles.

Whispersync Amazon's name for the process of keeping each of the books you are reading updated with your current page, bookmarks, notes and so on, across multiple devices or Kindle reading applications.

Wi-fi or **Wifi** Once colloquial, but now a generally accepted term for wireless networking. It embodies several standards, of which the four most common are 802.11a, 802.11b, 802.11g and 802.11n. The 'a' and 'g' variants can each achieve a maximum data throughput of 54 megabits per second, while 802.11b runs at 11 megabits per second. 802.11n, the fastest standard at 248 megabits per second, is as yet unratified, although draft standards have allowed it to be built into many wireless devices already, giving it good overall industry support. The Kindle uses 802.11b, g and n for the broad compatibility.

Windows The world's most commonly-used desktop and laptop operating system. Can be used to manage the Kindle, in which it appears like an external hard drive with connected using USB.

Wireless Access Point Hardware device that connects to your network or broadband connection and replicates the features of wired networks in a wireless form to provide network and Internet access to wifi devices such as the Kindle.

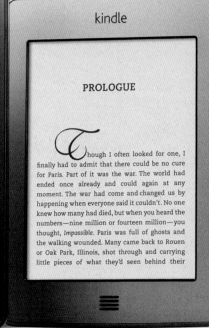

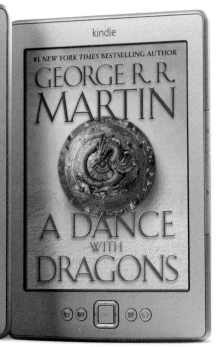